THE EPISTLES OF JOHN

Light, Love, Life

THE

EPISTLES OF JOHN

Light, Love, Life

BY

W. E. VINE, M.A.

ZONDERVAN
PUBLISHING HOUSE

OF THE ZONDERVAN CORPORATION | GRAND RAPIDS. MICHIGAN 49506

Published by special agreement with
Oliphants, Ltd.

U.S.A. Paperback Edition 1970

Second printing 1971
Third printing   1972
Fourth printing 1973

Library of Congress Catalog Card No. 73-136355

Printed in the United States of America

CONTENTS

THE FIRST EPISTLE OF JOHN

THE SECOND EPISTLE OF JOHN

THE THIRD EPISTLE OF JOHN

INTRODUCTION

One of the special objects for which this Epistle was written was to counteract the errors of the Gnostics. There were three sects whose heretical teachings began to influence the churches in the latter part of the first century: the Ebionites, followers of Ebion, who denied the Deity of Christ, teaching that He was merely a creature; the Docetists, who denied the humanity of Christ, teaching that He was merely a visionary being, a phantom, void of corporeal nature, and that He had not come in flesh; and the Cerinthians, followers of Cerinthus, who denied the union of the two natures in Christ, *i.e.*, the human and the Divine, prior to His baptism. The Apostle therefore sets forth the truth relating to both the essential Deity of Christ, and to His true humanity.

The second great object of the Epistle was to make clear to the readers the distinguishing features which characterize those who are born of God in contrast to those which mark the children of the evil one. These characteristics centre round three great truths concerning God:

    (1) God is Light (chapters 1 and 2),

    (2) God is Love (chapters 3 to 5: 5),

    (3) God is Life (chapter 5: 6 to end).

The children of God have fellowship with Him in respect of each of these, in contrast to those who are not born of God.

(1) Light symbolically stands for righteousness. Those who have fellowship with God do righteousness "as He is righteous." Sin is spiritual darkness, and is utterly incompatible with fellowship with God.

(2) Fellowship with God, in regard to His nature as love, produces love one toward another, in contrast to the spirit which was manifest in Cain and continues in the world.

(3) The "life" which God imparts is in His Son. Associated with this is the witness which each believer has in himself. Idolatry is incompatible with it.

CHAPTER I

ANALYSIS OF CHAPTER I

NOTES

Chapter I.   Verses 1–10

VERSE 1. **That which was from the beginning,**—This phrase is to be compared and contrasted with the opening words of the Gospel of John. In the Gospel he says "In the beginning was the Word." This does not imply that Christ was originated. What the Apostle is there setting forth is His eternal pre-existence, as possessed of Diety. Wherever a beginning is in view there Christ was, having been pre-existent to it. Before creation, for instance, He was with God, and was Himself God. Here in the Epistle the same thought attaches to the phrase "the beginning," but the Apostle sets forth Christ as having come into human experience from the eternity of the past. Having been pre-existent He became manifested. Neither in the Gospel nor in the Epistle does he open with the phrase "that which came to be", which would imply that Christ had a beginning. He did not begin to be, He essentially "was." This statement at once combats one of the great errors of the Gnostics, who regarded Christ as impersonal, a mere emanation. On the contrary the Apostles had themselves been in intimate contact with His Person.

that which we have heard, that which we have seen with our eyes, that which we beheld, and our hands handled,—This expresses a progress of experience in relation to Christ. It suggests a deepening degree of intimacy. One may hear a person without seeing him, may see him without close contemplation of his person, may behold him without handling him. The perfect tenses "have seen", "have heard", signify the abiding effect of the experiences. The aorist, or point, tenses, "beheld", "handled", mark the definiteness of the events referred to in the personal contact of the Apostles with the Lord.

concerning the Word of life;—This phrase gives the immediate subject about which the Apostle is writing. The accurate rendering of the R.V., "concerning", removes the ambiguity of the A.V. "of." The writer is not relating what he has seen or heard of Christ, but is intimating the subject of his Epistle. As in the Gospel, "the Word" is the Personal Word. John's use of the word *logos* is entirely to be distinguished from the use made of it by Philo of Alexandria and his school of philosophy in the second century, B.C. With them the *logos* was an impersonal idea, conveying the thoughts of God. The teachings of Philo had exercised a great influence upon Jewish thought, and had found their way into Gnostic teachings. Cerinthus taught the pagan doctrine of the existence of æons and emanations from the eternal God, and declared that Jesus of Nazareth was the natural son of Joseph and Mary and that the æon Christ came upon Him at His baptism and left Him before His crucifixion; that by this æon He wrought His miracles and taught; that only the man Jesus was crucified, not Jesus Christ. The Apostle lifts the word *logos* out of the sphere of speculative philosophy and establishes the truth that Jesus Christ, the Word, the *Logos*, was one with the Father, eternal in the Godhead, and, having taken human flesh, had become man, His Deity and humanity being thenceforward indissociable.

"The Word of life" combines the two truths that He is Himself life and that He imparts it, as the life (John 14: 6), He is the personal expression of what God is, the interpreter of His nature (cp. John 1: 18); but, as He also Himself said, He came that they might have life (John 10: 10).

VERSE 2.   and the life was manifested,—This verse, while parenthetic, confirms and expands the statements in verse 1, stressing the personality of "the Word of Life."

and we have seen, and bear witness, and declare unto you the life,— The order of these statements is noticeable:

(1) Personal experience,
(2) Public testimony,
(3) Particular proclamation to the saints.

the eternal life, which was with the Father, and was manifested unto us;—Three facts are pointed out:

(1) The unoriginated existence of the Person. This is intimated in the repetition of the word "the life," with the addition of "eternal."

(2) His Godhood in relation to the Father. The word *pros*, "with", as in the first verse of the Gospel, signifies not merely an accompaniment, but a living, active relation to, and communion with, the Father.

(3) His manifestation through His Incarnation.

These opening statements of the Epistle are convincing evidence of the authenticity of the Apostolic testimony as recorded in the New Testament. There is complete absence of aiming at originality or concoction. They are plain, simple declarations of facts of experience, and bear the marks of genuineness.

VERSE 3. **that which we have seen and heard declare we unto you also, that ye also may have fellowship with us:**—Verse 1 states the subject, verse 2 facts about the subject, verse 3 the purpose in view. This verse recalls the evidences afforded to sight and hearing as to the incarnation and manifestation of Him Who is the Word of life. But this is also added, that the life was manifested not merely to reveal God but to bring the redeemed into relationship with Him; for the particular kind of fellowship is now specified in this respect. The word *koinōnia* "fellowship", signifies "a having in common", "a sharing with". The high degree of the privilege of this fellowship is pointed out as follows:

yea, and our fellowship is with the Father, and with His Son Jesus Christ:—There is very strong emphasis on the word "our." This might be brought out in the following way: "The fellowship which is ours (that which distinguishes what believers have in common, in contrast to any other form of fellowship), is with the Father, and with His Son Jesus Christ."

The repetition of the preposition "with" marks a distinction between the Father and the Son, yet what the Apostle has said shows that the Father and Son are one in Godhood.

Here the Personal name "Jesus" is now introduced, identifying "the Word of life", "the eternal life", with the well-known Person who is the Son of the Father. The order of the titles is noticeable, the order "Jesus Christ" indicates that the One who dwelt on earth and died (Jehovah the Saviour) is also the exalted One, "the Christ of God".

VERSE 4. **and these things we write unto you, that our joy may be fulfilled.**—This expresses the second object which the Apostle has in view. "Our joy" is the joy of both writer and readers. There is a joy which is only fulfilled when we enter into practical fellowship with the Father and with the Son. "Fulfil" is very characteristic of John's writings (see John 3: 29; 7: 8; 12: 38; 15: 11; 16: 24; 17: 13; 2 John 12; Rev. 3: 2; 6: 11). Augustine's statement about joy is worth quoting here: "For there is a joy which is not given to the ungodly, that of all those who love Thee for Thine own sake, whose joy Thou Thyself art; and this is the happy life, to rejoice in Thee, of Thee. This is it! And there is no other."

VERSE 5. **And this is the message which we have heard from Him, and announce unto you,**—This is an extension of the declarations made in verses 1-3. The R.V. rendering "from Him" is important (in contrast to the A.V. "of Him") which tends to convey the meaning "about Him." Apostolic testimony was not given second hand. What the Apostles gave was not by hearsay, but was received directly from their Lord. John's statement is set in sharp contrast to the various deductions of the Gnostic teachers.

that God is light, and in Him is no darkness at all.—This brings us again to the three great statements of the Apostle concerning God as Light, Love and Life (see Introduction). His attribute of light is here represented as the basis of fellowship. He is not merely the light, nor a light, He *is* Light. Cp. John 1: 4 and the similar statement in 1 John 4: 8, 16, that "God is love." In the Gospel the Apostle shows that the life and the light are inseparable. Light is an essential condition of life. There, however, he says, "the Life was the Light of men" (John 1: 4). In the Epistle he shows, not so much the connection between light and life, but what it is to be in moral and spiritual darkness, without fellowship with Him. Hence the double statement, one positive and the other negative "God is light, and in Him is no darkness at all." (Cp. the similar double statement in 1: 3.)

VERSE 6. **If we say that we have fellowship with Him, and walk in the darkness, we lie, and do not the truth:**—This is the first of seven clauses introduced by "if" in the two sections from 1: 5 to 2: 6. The conditions thus laid down serve to distinguish actual possession from mere profession. There is an intimation of what the Apostle develops more fully in the body of the Epistle, namely, the distinguishing mark which differentiates the children of God from the children of the Devil (see 3: 10). In this passage the distinction is between walking in darkness and walking in the light. The former is the condition of the unregenerate, the latter of those who are related to Him who is Light (v. 5). To walk in the light we must be partakers of His nature. The word rendered "walk" suggests the habitual or constant course of life.

The combined statements, "we lie, and do not tell the truth," are significant. The truth is not merely a creed. It is always that which has a bearing upon the life. The truth is doctrine "according to God" that is, it is consistent with His character. Right action is an expression of the truth, and those who walk according to the truth thereby express the character of God. Hence the contrast in the next verse. Note the corresponding clauses in this verse:

(a) "we lie" is set in contrast to "if we say;"
(b) "and do not the truth" corresponds to "walk in darkness."

VERSE 7. **but if we walk in the light, as He is in the light, we have fellowship one with another,**—There is first union and then communion. There cannot be the latter without the former. To be walking in the light as He is in the light is both to have relationship with God and to live in a manner corresponding to the relationship.

Thus far the main subjects of the Epistle are "the way, the truth and the life", for walking suggests the way. Note the contrast between "we walk" and "He is"; our life here is transient; God dwells in eternity.

The "fellowship with one another" is the fellowship of believers with each other, though that is the evidence and expression of fellowship with God. For the further use of "one another" in this Epistle see 3: 11; 3: 23; 4: 7; 4: 11; 4: 12; see also 2 John 5—seven occasions in the two Epistles. This fellowship is the outcome of walking in the light. There was no fellowship for the Egyptians in the plague of darkness.

and the blood of Jesus His Son cleanseth us from all sin.—This is the second result of walking in the light. For the use of the single name Jesus, see also 2: 22; 4: 3 (R.V.); 4: 15; 5: 1; 5: 5, "Jesus" is His human name; "His Son" is His eternal relationship. The heretic Cerinthus taught that Jesus was a mere man when His blood was shed, and the Ebionites taught that He was a mere man from His birth to His death. The Apostle testifies to the contrary. The blood was not that of one who was merely human.

"The Name 'Jesus' brings out His human nature, in which He assumed a real body of flesh and blood, which blood was shed for us. The blood stands for the life, for the life of the flesh is in the blood. Sin has forfeited the life. Christ's life, yielded by the sheddings of His blood, has brought life to those who, having forfeited their life by sin, accept Him as their Saviour on the ground of His Death" (Westcott). His blood is both available and efficacious. It is efficacious because Jesus is the Son of God. John speaks of believers as "children of God", reserving the title "son" for Christ. In Paul's Epistles they are spoken of as both "sons" and "children". The present tense "cleanseth" does not convey the thought of fresh applications of the blood of Christ to believers; the meaning is that sin is removed by God on the ground of the once offered sacrifice of Christ. His blood stands for His expiatory death in the shedding of His blood. In Scripture the shedding of the blood signifies the taking, or with regard to Christ, the giving, of the life. Whenever God forgives sin he does so on that basis (v. 9). Cp. the language of Heb. 9: 14, 25; Rev. 7: 14. Cleansing would seem to be additional to forgiveness. The blood of Christ sanctifies as well as justifies, changes a character as well as relieves the conscience. For the practical walk in the light, as well as for our standing in it, our only fitness is through the full and lasting virtue of the blood of Christ.

Verse 8. Profession of sinlessness—self deceit—void of truth.

Verse 9. Confession of sin—Divine cleansing—void of condemnation.

Verse 10. Denial of sin—dishonour to God—void of revelation.

VERSE 8.   **If we say that we have no sin,**—Not the committal of sin is in view here, but the principle of sin; yet not merely what is called original sin, but sin in the general sense, sin of every description.

we deceive ourselves,—*i.e.* "we lead ourselves astray;" "ourselves" bears emphasis. On the one hand, we neither deceive God nor our neighbours, and, on the other hand, we do ourselves what Satan seeks to do for us (Rev. 12: 9; 20: 10). We are responsible for the error.

and the truth is not in us.—This is an advance upon verse 6, a worse condition than "not doing truth." The truth is "the body of Christian doctrine", the revealed counsels and will of God, communicated to our hearts by His Spirit. To claim sinlessness is to be void of that revelation, just as to walk in the darkness is to fail to do those things by which the truth is translated into the life.

VERSE 9. **If we confess our sins,**—This, being set in contrast to verse 8, suggests that there sin in general is in view. Instead, however, of saying, "If we say we have sin, etc", the Apostle states what is fuller, stronger and more progressive. Confession, *i.e.* of specific sins, is evidence of sincerity; it is not a statement of mere profession; it ¡ ₁volves seeking forgiveness. The confession is plainly to God, and not to men.

He is faithful and righteous—This is set in contrast to "we deceive ourselves"; the direct contrast would be "we are true", but that is replaced by the more important statement of the attributes and mercy of God. It is with God that we have to do. His two attributes are here combined to provide an adequate conception of His nature. Righteous is the state of being right; in His faithfulness He is consistent with His character; in acting righteously He is faithful to His own nature. His righteousness stands in contrast with "all unrighteousness" (end of the verse) and is in line with "Jesus Christ the righteous" (2: 1). Cp. Rev. 3: 14, and Jer. 42: 5, where the Septuagint has "righteous and faithful."

to forgive us our sins,—God's acts are in absolute harmony with His purposes. His purpose is that His faithfulness and righteousness should be exhibited in forgiving our sins and cleansing us from all unrighteousness. That God forgives and cleanses, and is righteous in doing so (and He can never be anything else but righteous), is a mark of His faithfulness to His own character. The word rendered "forgive" is, lit., to send away, which is also the lit. meaning of "remit." The same word is in 2: 12; cp. the language of Lev. 16: 10, R.V., "to send him away", and verse 21, in reference to the scapegoat.

and to cleanse us from all unrighteousness.—While remission has reference to sinful acts, cleansing from unrighteousness has to do with the personal character of the sinner. There is thus a double result of confession, deliverance from the guilt of sin, and purification from its pollution.

Unrighteousness (*adikia*) is the negation of what is consistent with God's character; sin (*hamartia*, v. 8) is lit. the missing of the mark.

VERSE 10.   **If we say that we have not sinned,**—The third kind of false protestation; the first (v. 6) is a denial of the distinction between spiritual light and darkness, the second (v. 8) is a denial of the sinfulness of our nature, the third is a denial of sins committed—themselves the effect of a sinful state.

we make Him a liar,—*i.e.*, what we say is entirely inconsistent with God's character. He has declared that "all have sinned" (Rom. 3:23). To make Him a liar is worse than lying (v. 6) or self-deceit (v. 8). To profess not to have sinned is to deny the facts of human nature and the need of a Redeemer, and to impugn both the character of God and the whole scheme of His redemptive work.

and His word is not in us.—This is parallel to "the truth is not in us" (v. 8). His word (*logos*) is the truth in the concrete form of the Scriptures, the inspired utterances of God's mind.

The "if we say" of verses 6 and 8 is in each case followed by a contrasting condition of the happy realities of the Christian experience (verses 7 and 9). This third "if we say" is not so followed. The reason is that what might be expected to follow is already covered by verse 9.

CHAPTER II

ANALYSIS OF CHAPTER II

(A) VERSES 1–12—ADDRESSED TO ALL BELIEVERS

(B) VERSES 13–27—ADDRESSED, IN A TWOFOLD MESSAGE, TO THE THREE BRANCHES OF THE HEAVENLY FAMILY

(C) VERSE 28—ADDRESSED TO ALL BELIEVERS

(A)   Verses 1–12

	Verses
(1) Sinning	1, 2
(a) The avoidance—the purpose of John's writing	1a
(b) The remedy—an Advocate	1b, 2
1. The Person with whom He acts	
2. The Name of the Advocate	
3. The character of the Advocate	
4. The nature of His advocacy	
5. The subjects of His advocacy	
(2) Knowledge of God	3–5a
(a) The assurance and its condition	3
(b) The profession and its denial	4
(c) The fulfilment and its effect (p. 5).	
(3) Abiding in Christ	5b, 6
(a) The assurance	5b
(b) The condition	6
(4) The Commandment, old and new	7, 8
(a) When it was given	7
(b) In what it consisted	
(c) Its character	8
1. The condition—in Him, in you	
2. The reason—the shining of the light	

(B)   Verses 13–27

(C)   Verse 28

(*Note.*—The word rendered "little children," in vv. 1, 12 and 28, is different from that so rendered in vv. 13 and 18. The latter represents the young converts (*paidia*), and is set in contrast to the fathers and young men. In the former the address is not to one branch of the family of God but to all the readers, *i.e.*, to believers in general. All such are "little children" (*teknia*). The passage including vv. 13-27 is thus parenthetic.)

Chapter II.   Verses 1–28

Introductory Note

The subject of the first chapter is closely continued. The fact that believers do sin is now followed by an exhortation not to do so, and by a statement of the remedy when sin is committed. Hence the value of the Person of Christ and the efficiency of His work (vv. 1, 2). This leads to the condition required for personal acquaintance with Christ and the inconsistency of a profession of this knowledge and nonconformity to His commandments (vv. 3, 4). In contrast to this is the practical experience of intimate relationship with Christ produced by the perfecting of the love of God in the fulfilment of His World (v. 5). The passage closes with an exhortation to back up profession with consistent conduct.

(A)   Verses 1–12

VERSE 1.   **My little children,**—Teknia, a diminutive term, expressive not of immaturity but of endearment. The same word is in vv. 12, and 28, but not the same in vv. 13 and 18 (see above).

these things write I unto you, that ye may not sin.—This refers to what he has just been saying. His insistence on the facts of sinfulness and sins, and the remedy provided, is not to be taken as conveying any intimation of the inevitableness of sin. On the contrary his teaching is to be preventative against sinning.

The aorist, or point, tense in "that ye may not sin" shows that each act of sin is to be avoided. Contrast the continuous present tenses, *e.g.*, in 1: 3, "that ye may have fellowship."

And if any man sin,—The aorist tense again, as in the preceding verse, indicating a distinct act. We might have expected this clause to begin with "But". The "and" suggests the connection "And that ye may know that if any man sin."

we have an Advocate with the Father,—Paraklētos, our English word "paraclete," is used only by the Apostle John in the New Testament, four times in the Gospel (14: 16, 26; 15: 26; 16: 7) and here only in his Epistles. It literally signifies one who is "called to one's side," and hence one who acts as an advocate, undertaking another's cause. As the corresponding noun *paraklēsis*, "comfort", "exhortation", shows, it has the extended meaning to signify the act of consoling or supporting. There is a difference in context between this passage and those in the Gospel. Here the word has to do with the question of sin; there, where it is used of both Christ and the Holy Spirit, it more especially refers to solace and support, and so is rightly rendered "Comforter." As a High Priest the Lord Jesus deals with guilt; as an Advocate He effects restoration. Sin interrupts communion, which is restored through His advocacy.

He is our Advocate "with the Father." The preposition "with" is the same as in 1: 2, and signifies one who not only is in the Father's presence but whose attitude is directed towards Him on our behalf. The reference to God as "the Father" recalls what was said in 1: 2, 3.

The Apostle does not say "If any man sin, he has an Advocate," but "we have", putting himself on the same level with his readers, all alike being in need. The Apostles never assumed the position of priests acting on behalf of the laity.

Jesus Christ the righteous:—The order of the titles suggests that the one Who came to us through His death (Jesus) is in the presence of the Father as the Anointed One (Christ) in all the efficacy of His finished work and in the perfection of His character. The efficacy of His ministry is guaranteed by the righteousness of His Person. His righteousness is set in contrast to our sin. Cp. 1: 9.

VERSE 2. **and He is the propitiation for our sins;**—The pronoun "He" bears emphasis and we might render by "He Himself." The word *hilasmos* is used here and in 4: 10 alone in the New Testament. It signifies expiation. In Num. 5: 8 the LXX has "the ram of the propitiation", and in Psa. 130: 4, "With Thee is the propitiation" (*hilasmos*, in each place). It denotes the ground upon which God shows mercy to the guilty. Christ Himself, and He alone, is this, through His Death, in the shedding of His blood in sacrifice. Two things are therefore indicated (1) the finished work of the Cross, (2) the value of the Living Person.

Not only was He the Propitiator by offering Himself, He is in His own Person the Propitiation. This is connected very closely with what has preceded. That He is the propitiation is what gives perfect effect to His advocacy, and thus the statement presents the abiding results of His atoning sacrifice for our sins. Cp. Heb. 2: 17, R.V., "to make propitiation." Such phrases as "propitiating God" and "reconciling God" are foreign to the New Testament. God shows mercy through Christ, and man is the one to be reconciled, Rom. 5: 10; 2 Cor. 5: 18.

and not for ours only, but also for the whole world.—The little connecting word in the original, rendered "and", does not serve to add a new idea, so much as to counteract an erroneous teaching as to the application of the propitiation. The provision made by the sacrifice of Christ extends to the whole world, yet the actual effect is not universal. The whole world lies within the scope of the propitiation, no one being necessarily excluded from its benefits. The only exclusion is on the part of those who will not avail themselves of it. For the universality of the provision cp. 4: 14, and John 1: 20; 3: 16, Nothing is served by the italicized addition in the A.V., "the sins of".

VERSE 3.   **And hereby know we that we know Him,**—This forms a transition to a fresh line of thought, that of keeping God's commandments. This, however, is connected with the subject, in the first chapter, of fellowship with God. Now the subject of the knowledge of God is introduced, and both the obedience and the knowledge are the result of the propitiation. Note the parallel, in inverse, or chiasmic, order:

> (*a*) If we walk in the light,
>   (*b*) We have fellowship.
>   (*c*) The Blood cleanses.
>   (*c*) He is the propitiation.
>   (*b*) We know that we know Him,
> (*a*) If we keep His commandments.

The tenses of the verb differ in the two parts of the sentence. The first is present continuous, expressing a course of procedure, the second is a perfect tense, expressing completeness. To bring this out, we may paraphrase thus: "hereby we constantly have the experience of knowing that we have come to know Him." For further instances of the continuous tense of this word see 2: 5, 18, 29; 3: 1, 19, 24; 4: 2, 6, 7 (not v. 8), 13, 16; 5: 2 (not vv. 13, 15, 18, 19, 20). The word is *ginōskō*, *i.e.*, "to learn by experience", and this is to be distinguished from *oida*, used in the verses mentioned in brackets, which means "to know by immediate knowledge, or by intuition".

The above references serve to show that "to know" is one of the characteristic words of this Epistle, and suggests a contrast to the false knowledge professed by the Gnostics.

The "Him" may refer either to the Father, v. 1, or to the Son, v. 2. A comparison with 3: 23, as to the commandments, would point to the Father. The Apostle speaks of knowing the Father (2: 13), the Son (2: 14) and the Holy Spirit (4: 2).

if we keep His commandments.—Neither fellowship with, nor knowledge of, God can exist apart from obedience to His will. The Gnostic teaching that intellectual attainment is man's highest good, finds here its refutation. Nor, again, as is shown later, is knowledge combined with emotional sentiment available. Peter went so far with his "Thou knowest that I love Thee", the Lord led him further. Devotion is realized in obedience. Keeping His commandments is a matter of holiness of life, moral conduct, walking in the light. Only so do we really know God, and prove it to ourselves as well as to Him.

VERSE 4. **He that saith, I know Him, and keepeth not His commandments, is a liar, and the truth is not in him;**—A comparison should here be made with 1:6 and might be set out as follows:

1:6

(*a*) If we say that we have fellowship with Him,
(*b*) And walk in the darkness,
(*c*) We lie and do not the truth.

2:4

(*a*) He that saith, I know Him,
(*b*) And keepeth not His Commandments,
(*c*) Is a liar and the truth is not in Him.

A comparison may further be made with parallel clauses in 1:6, 8 and 10. The Apostle increases the forcefulness of His statement concerning the iniquity of mere profession without conformity in the life, till he here reaches the greatest pitch of severity. In such inconsistency—

(*a*) A person does not the truth—1:6
(*b*) The truth is not in Him—1:8
(*c*) He makes God a liar—1:10
(*d*) He is a liar himself and in him the truth is not.

He is not merely guilty of certain statements and acts of falsehood, but is himself false in his moral state. The order, too, in the last sentence is more emphatic than in 1:8. There it was "truth is not in us"; here it is "and in this man truth is not."

VERSE 5. **but whoso keepeth His word,**—Here the stress is on "keepeth"; in v. 4 it was on "commandments". His word (*logos*) is the whole, of which His commandments are the parts. It is the complete Divine revelation.

in Him verily hath the love of God been perfected.—The love of God is a comprehensive phrase, to be taken in its fullest sense. It is not merely objective, love to God; that is but the counterpart of the love of God to us (subjective); the one is the answer to the other. The love evinced by the believer finds its source in, and derives its nature from, God's love.

Thus here "the love of God" is the exercise of God's love manifesting itself in the human heart and life in practical love towards God and our fellow men. This is confirmed in 4: 10, 11. Love is the fulfilling of God's commandments, which are summed up in the one commandment concerning love, and in the fulfilment of this the love of God is (or has been) perfected in us. Love has thus attained to its end. Selfishness and carnal desires are banished, and the will of God is carried out both in us and through us towards others. The perfect tense thus expresses the abiding effects produced by God's love and the response to it in our heart.

In this statement the Apostle characteristically presents the positive side of what He said in v. 4; just as v. 4 presented the opposite to the statement in v. 3. Accordingly vv. 3 and 5 are associated in teaching. They are not different ways of presenting the same thing. Rather, they present inseparably connected experiences, namely, the enjoyment of the knowledge of God, the keeping of His commandments, the keeping of His Word and the perfecting of His love in us.

We might have expected the Apostle to say "whoso keepeth His Word, in him verily the truth is", to correspond to what he has just stated. He says instead, "in him verily hath the love of God been perfected"; this emphasizes, not some personal trait in the believer, but rather the work of Divine love in Him and through Him as the sphere of its operation.

Hereby know we that we are in Him:—The Apostle has spoken of having fellowship with God and of knowing God. Now he goes further and speaks of being "in Him." This is one of the great central truths of the Christian faith. Introduced here in the Epistle it is taken up in various ways subsequently. It is also especially brought out in the Gospel; compare, *e.g.*, 14: 20; 15: 4; 17: 10, 21,

23. The condition of being "in Him" is not a matter of absorption into Deity, as Pantheism teaches, but of spiritual relationship and unity of life, which involves the removal of the alienation of man in his unregenerate state from God, and the enjoyment of fellowship with God and oneness with Him in His will and purpose.

The "hereby" may refer to "whoso keepeth His Word" at the beginning of the verse. More probably, however, the R.V. is correct in connecting it, as a fresh sentence, with v. 6; just as the "hereby" in v. 3 referred to what immediately followed.

For "know we" see the note above on v. 3. The assurance is not by way of contrast to doubt, but is simply a statement of a constantly enjoyed experience.

VERSE 6. **he that saith he abideth in Him ought himself also to walk even as He walked.**—Abiding in Christ suggests the thought of habitual fellowship as the result of being in Him (see the end of the preceding verse). "To abide" is another word characterizing John's writings. It is rendered in seven different ways in our English Version. There would be some advantage in adhering to the one rendering.

The word *opheilō*, rendered "ought", suggests the thought of a debt, and so of moral responsibility, a duty incumbent upon the one who makes the profession. The responsibility is to walk "even as" Christ walked, the "even as" suggesting the closest conformity to Him in character and conduct.

The tense of the word "walked" is the aorist, which, in contrast to the imperfect (which would signify a custom or habit), here presents a single and complete view of the Lord's activity in the days of His flesh, as a life of the perfect fulfilment of the will of God.

With this insistence (a stern blow against Gnostic antinomianism) the Apostle brings to a close and rounds off the teaching of the first part of his Epistle. In the first chapter he spoke of walking in the light as He is in the light, and the blessings resulting therefrom; here, at the close, the thought is carried on to the walk of Christ Himself and the obligation to be conformed to Him. The Epistle thus far presents, on the one hand, for those who are genuine believers, the joy and comfort of the rich provision that God has made in Christ for them to meet all their needs, and, on the other hand, to the mere professor, the terrible nature of profession without practice.

Having shown that to walk in the light is to walk in fellowship with God and with one another (1: 5–7), and involves, on the one hand, both consciousness of sin and confession of it (1: 8–10), and, on the other hand, the keeping of God's commandments and a walk in conformity to that of Christ (2: 6), the Apostle, extending his subject, now shows that this further involves brotherly love.

VERSE 7. **Beloved,**—A new mode of address in the Epistle (not "Brethren," as the A.V.), and appropriate to the subject of "the love of God" in the preceding verse, and to that of love to one another, in the section now beginning.

no new commandment write I unto you, but an old commandment which ye had from the beginning:—The R.V. gives the correct order of the clauses, and thus preserves the due emphasis, as the point of the verse lies in the contrast between the old and the new. In the preceding section he had spoken of commandments. This is now changed to the singular, "commandment", and for this reason, that as the subject is now to be that of brotherly love the commandments are summed up in the one law of love; "love is the fulfilling of the law."

This is the commandment which was fulfilled in the walk and teaching of Christ, and which, as the Apostle intimates, he himself had handed on to the converts from the very beginning of his testimony. The word *kainos*, "new," signifies what is fresh, in contrast to that which is familiar and well known. Another word, *neos*, "new", differs from *kainos*, in that it marks a contrast to what is old, hence it is often rendered "young." John uses it once only in his writings, in John 21: 18, whereas he uses *kainos* fourteen times.

Similarly there are two distinctive words for "old", *palaios*, which is the word in the present passage, and which signifies old in time, whereas *archaios*, signifies old in character. John uses *archaios* twice only in his writings, and in each in reference to the Devil, as a serpent (Rev. 12: 9; 20: 2). The commandment to which he refers here was something old in time. It was given under the Law of Sinai. The believers had had it from the beginning, that is, from the beginning of the testimony given to them.

the old commandment is the word which ye heard.—The addition "from the beginning" in the A.V. is not in the best MSS. Its omission gives the due force to "the word." The "word" stands for the commandment and signifies all the teaching concerning the commandment.

"Heard" is in the aorist, or point tense, not the perfect, as in the A.V. and this confirms what was said above, that "the beginning" in the previous sentence signifies the beginning of the testimony given to the readers.

VERSE 8.   **Again, a new commandment write I unto you, which thing is true in Him and in you;**—The "again" introduces another view of what has just been said. The command, which was in one sense old but not antiquated, was also new in the fresh sanction which it had received and because the Holy Spirit had been given to dwell in the hearts of the children of God, enabling them to fulfil it.

"which thing" indicates the love which is enjoined by the commandment. That it is *"true"* signifies that it receives its fulfilment, is made good. It was (and is) true *"in Him"*, as not only had the commandment been given by Him but it had also been exhibited in His example. It is also true in the children of God because it is to be received and fulfilled by them. It is to be noticed that the preposition "in" is repeated; the Apostle does not say "in Him and you"; a distinction is necessary; not only was Christ the living embodiment of it, He reissued the commandment. Believers are to fulfil it for they are to walk even as He walked, but they have not originated the commandment; yet both in Him and in them its truth is exhibited. Verse 8 is to be connected with v. 6.

because the darkness is passing away, and the true light already shineth.—The teaching and example of Christ, which make the old commandment new, and which are having their fulfilment in those who walk even as He walked, are consequent upon the shining of the true Light, with the accompanying effect that the darkness is passing away. Christ himself is "the Light of men" (John 1: 4), the Light that, coming into the world, "lighteth every man" (John 1: 9).

That the true light had been shining *"already"* signifies that it had for some time been shining, not that it had been shining sooner than might have been expected.

The coming of the Holy Spirit with his illuminating power into the heart of the believer causing him to walk in love as Christ did, expels the darkness. As men are being brought into the light and become the followers of Christ, so the darkness is passing away. That seems to be the significance of the continuous tense. For the confirmation of this see v. 9. Literally it is "the light, the true light, is already shining." This stresses its character as true. The word "true" is *alēthinon*, and is thus somewhat different from *alēthēs* in the preceding part of the verse. *Alēthēs* is the true as opposed to the spurious; it signifies the genuine, and is illustrated in the old English word "very," as, *e.g.*, in the phrase "very God of very God",—not the true God as opposed to false gods, but God genuinely as such, God as a fact, a reality. Here the true light signifies Christ Himself, cp. John 1: 9.

VERSE 9. **He that saith he is in the light, and hateth his brother, is in the darkness even until now.**—This is the fifth occasion upon which the Apostle speaks of inconsistency between profession and conduct. The first is a profession of fellowship with God (1: 6); the second a profession of sinlessness (1: 8); the third that of abstinence from sin (1: 10); the fourth that of the knowledge of God (2: 4); the fifth that of being in the light (2: 9). There is a sixth in 4: 20. The contrasts are light and darkness, truth and falsehood, love and hate. Walking in light, in truth, and in love constitutes fellowship with God.

From the general scope of the Epistle, it seems probable that by "his brother" the Apostle is referring to the members of the family of God. As a matter of principle, however, the teaching of Christ is that love is to be shown to all men and not hatred (see Matt. 5: 44; 1 Cor. 13: 2). Yet the context of the Epistle and its general teaching would seem to show that the spiritual relationship is under immediate consideration here. See especially chap. 3: 13–17.

The phrase "even until now" is to be connected with the statement in v. 8, that the true light already shineth. One who hates his brother, so far from being in the light, has not yet received it.

VERSE 10. **He that loveth his brother abideth in the light, and there is none occasion of stumbling in him.**—Note the three phrases, "walking in the light" (1: 7); "being in the light" (2: 9); "abiding in the light" (2: 10). Walking speaks of conduct, abiding speaks of the condition which determines the conduct.

It is possible, as a matter of translation, to render by "there is no occasion of stumbling in it," that is, in the light; and the contrast to this is that one who hates his brother does not know where he is going. The whole context, however, seems to confirm the rendering "in him".

As to whether the reference is to causing others to stumble, or stumbling oneself, while it is quite true that he who hates his brother sets a bad example, and might cause others to sin, yet there is nothing in the passage to indicate that this is the meaning. On the contrary, what is under consideration is the direct spiritual condition of the person himself. This is, moreover, confirmed by the parallel phrase in v. 4, "the truth is not in him", and, as to walking in the light, cp. John 11: 9, 10, "If a man walk in the day, he stumbleth not, because he seeth the light of this world. But if a man walk in the night, he stumbleth, because the light is not in him." Cp. Psa. 119: 165.

VERSE 11. **But he that hateth his brother is in the darkness, and walketh in the darkness, and knoweth not whither he goeth, because the darkness hath blinded his eyes.**—This verse explains v. 9, and enforces its teaching by describing in a three-fold way the condition of the mere professor, who hates his brother. The three statements are as to:—

(1) His existence—he is in the darkness,
(2) His activity—he walks in the darkness,
(3) His blindness—he knows not whither he is going.

(1) Since he is in the darkness he is actually in separation from the children of light.

(2) His course of conduct is in the darkness, however varied his circumstances may be.

(3) Just as animals that are kept in the dark become blind, so the darkness of one who hates his brother blinds his eyes and prevents him from seeing where he is going—not merely his eventual destiny, but the very course he is pursuing. The organ that never exercises its function loses its power.

The article before the word "darkness" is to be observed, just as in the case of "the light"; the one is specifically set in contrast to the other; in each case the article is required in the rendering. Sometimes the article merely signifies that the noun is used in an abstract sense, but not so where what is referred to is specified, as in this Epistle.

While the word rendered "hath blinded" is in the aorist sense, it is a perfective aorist and is better rendered by the perfect tense in English. It points indeed to the initial oncoming of the blindness (hence the aorist), but combines the permanent effect also. The context is nearly always the guide as to whether the aorist signifies merely a past event or includes the effects of it.

The contrast between the true believer who is in the light and walks in the light, and the false professor who is in the darkness and walks in hatred, is now complete, so far as this passage goes. There is no neutral position. The distinction is important and bears upon a later passage in the Epistle, where the contrast between those who are children of God and those who are not is again set out. As Bengel says, "There is direct opposition. Where there is not love there is hatred. It may be latent but it is there."

VERSE 12. **I write unto you, my little children, because your sins are forgiven you for His Name's sake.**—This verse, which is sometimes taken as part of the next section, is to be regarded rather as a link between the two. The next section really begins with v. 13, and contains distinct addresses to three parts of the heavenly family, whereas v. 12 addresses all the children of God. This we shall notice more fully later. Verse 12 is thus to be associated with v. 1 of this chapter, where the Apostle addressed the whole family in the words "My little children." There he exhorted them against sinning, and pointed out the provision God had made in regard to sin. Here he reminds the true children of God that their sins are forgiven them for His Name's sake. While, then, v. 12 is linked with the beginning of the chapter, it forms at the same time a fitting close to what has immediately preceded, and points out what is especially true of those who are really children of God, in contrast to those who make a profession, but do not keep His commandments of love and therefore walk in darkness, and whose sins are not forgiven.

With the phrase, "for His Name's sake" cp. Psa. 23: 3; 25: 11; 31: 3; 79: 9; 109: 21; 143: 11; Jer. 14: 7, 11. Throughout the Scripture the Divine names are indicative of the attributes, character and ways of God. That anything should be done for His Name's sake signifies that the doing is consistent with His character and counsels. These have been embodied and revealed in the Lord Jesus Christ. This, then, is true in regard to God's forgiveness of our sins. The Name is to be associated both with the Father and with the Son, as in 1: 3, 7.

(B) Verses 13–27

In regard to the three parts of the family of God, whom the Apostle twice addresses in vv. 13-27, it is necessary to observe the distinction between the word *paidia*, rendered "little children", the youngest members of the family (vv. 13 and 18), and the word *teknia*, similarly rendered in our Versions in vv. 12 and 28, but denoting the whole family of God to whom the Apostle is writing his Epistle in general. *Teknia* is the word, for instance, in the first verse of chap. 2.

Verses 13 to 27, which we are now about to consider, practically form a break in the Epistle in this respect. The first address to the three members of the family is given in v. 13. The Fathers are again addressed at the beginning of v. 14; then the young men, in the same verse down to v. 17; then the little children—those who have been recently converted (vv. 18-27). After this the Apostle resumes his message to the whole of his readers and continues thus from v. 28 to the end of the Epistle.

VERSE 13. **I write unto you, fathers,**—Suggestive both of maturity and authority. They are the older men in the heavenly family, those who by reason of experience are looked up to for sympathy and guidance and assistance.

because ye know Him which is from the beginning.—The tense of the verb rendered "know" indicates that the knowledge has been gained as the fruit of experience; "ye know as the result of having come to know", the same tense as the second word "know" in v. 3. (See John 17: 3.) "Him which is from the beginning" is Christ, as in 1: 1. Notice the change from "that" to "Him". The purpose for which the Apostle used the former word does not exist in this part of the Epistle; hence the change to the personal pronoun.

I write unto you, young men,—Those who have reached, or who are nearing, the prime of life—those who have had some experience of the spiritual conflict.

because ye have overcome the Evil One.—Overcoming is a prominent subject in John's writings, especially in this Epistle and in Revelation. It is found six times in the Epistle and seventeen times in the Apocalypse. The perfect tense indicates the abiding results of past victories. There is of course no suggestion that there are not further conflicts in store.

The Evil One is Satan, who is thus described five times in this Epistle, here and in 2: 14; 3: 12; 5: 18, 19. The designation was evidently familiar to his readers. The word rendered "evil" is *poneros*, and differs from the more frequent and general word, *kakos*, "bad", in this, that, while *kakos* may simply mean what is evil in itself, *poneros* carries with it the idea of what is pernicious and acts detrimentally to others, not only evil (passively bad), but evilly disposed (actively harmful), whether in matters of false doctrine, or temptations in the moral sphere. The young men who are addressed have so far proved faithful, and have not yielded themselves to the corrupting influences around them.

I have written unto you, little children,—The change from "I write" to "I have written" is best explained as follows: When the Apostle says "I write", he is speaking of his being there and then engaged in the act of writing the Epistle. The tense of the verb rendered "I have written" is the *epistolary aorist*. In letter writing among the Greeks it was customary for the writer to project his thoughts to the time when the recipient, or recipients, would be reading the letter. From their point of view he "wrote" it a considerable time before they received it; accordingly he speaks of it in that way, having regard, not only to the completed letter, but to the time of its perusal by the readers. In English we do not use this tense with regard to letter writing. We should say "I am writing", but inasmuch as the present tense has already been used from that point of view it is best to do as the Revisers have done, and render it by "I have written." The "little children" are the babes in Christ.

because ye know the Father.—The tense of the verb rendered "ye know" is the same as in v. 13. The realization of the Fatherhood of God belongs to the youngest believer. The Spirit Himself bears witness with their spirit that they are the children of God (Rom 8: 16). The fathers have entered into the deeper truths relating to Christ as the centre of the Divine counsels. The babes have learned to cry "Abba, Father" because they have been born to God.

VERSE 14. **I have written unto you, fathers, because ye know Him which is from the beginning.**—There is nothing additional in the second address to the fathers. Yet it is not a mere repetition. There is the change from "I write" to "I have written", the significance of which has been explained in the note on the preceding verse. There is in the repetition, firstly, a suggestion of finality in regard to the subject of their knowledge, and secondly, an indication of satisfaction in the heart of the Apostle with the spiritual condition of the fathers.

I have written unto you, young men, because ye are strong, and the word of God abideth in you, and ye have overcome the Evil One.—In the case of the fathers the appeal was to their maturity and authority; with the young men it is to their energy and victory over temptation. The means of their victory is their strength, and the secret of their strength is the Word of God. For the Word of God is the revelation of His will and the means of receiving the fulness of Christ; it is likewise the all-sufficient counteractive against the errors of the time. In Eph. 6:17 the Word of God is spoken of as a weapon of attack, "the sword of the Spirit"; here it is an indwelling power, giving strength for victory over the Evil One. The effect therefore is the same in each passage. As in the introduction, in v. 13, which is here expanded, victory in the past leaves its permanent effects, but it is not in itself sufficient to ensure victory in the future; hence the Apostle has fresh injunctions to give.

VERSE 15. **Love not the world, neither the things that are in the world.**—There are four Greek words for "world" in the New Testament:

(1) *gē* the earth: it is distinguished from the heavens,
(2) *oikoumenē*, the inhabited world, the abode of men,
(3) *aiōn*, an age or generation, a lifetime, an era; it frequently signifies all that exists in the world as characterized by the conditions of an epoch,
(4) *kosmos*, the word used here, which literally denotes "the adorned thing." It signifies the sum total of,
  (*a*) the universe, or,
  (*b*) humanity viewed as a system,
  either (i) simply, the human race,
  or (ii) in an ethical sense, the sum total of human life considered in its alienation from, and hostility to, God.

That the Apostle passes at once to a warning against love of the world, after mentioning the Evil One, is suggestive of his power in and over the world. "The whole world lieth in the evil one" (5:19). He therefore uses this system of humanity, in its alienation from God,

That the Apostle passes at once to a warning against love of the world, after mentioning the Evil One, is suggestive of his power in and over the world. "The whole world lieth in the evil one" (5: 19). He therefore uses this system of humanity, in its alienation from God, as a means of enticing the believer from his attachment to Christ. There is no contradiction between this and the fact of God's love manifested towards the world, as mentioned in John 3: 16. The statement that "God so loved the world" refers to His attitude towards the human race simply as such. What the believer is not to love is the world as viewed in its antagonism to what is of God. Friendship with it is enmity against God (Jas. 4: 4, cp. 1: 27). Both in the Gospel of John and in the Epistle, the world and darkness stand almost for the same thing (see 1 John 2: 8 with 2: 17). To love the world which lies in the Evil One and yet to overcome the Evil One himself is impossible. The things that are in the world are the things which characterize it as such, and these are described in the next verse. By "the things that are in the world" are meant, not material objects, though these themselves may be the means of allurement, but rather those evil elements in it as a system of humanity in its opposition to God and His Christ, and its rejection of His claims. One does not prevent love of the world by entering upon a monastic life, or, on the other hand, by simply devoting oneself to good works. The effective power against the Evil One is love to God the Father and to Christ His Son. That and the love of the world are mutually antagonistic (cp. 6: 24).

If any man love the world, the love of the Father is not in him.— The primary significance here is not that such a person does not love the Father, but that the love of the Father is not the controlling principle of His life. The love of the Father is that which, being in the believer, produces in him a responding love, a devoted recognition of His grace and His claims. In v. 5 the Apostle spoke of the love of God. Here, where the family relationship is particularly in view, he speaks of "the love of the Father."

VERSE 16. **For all that is in the world,**—This verse confirms the preceding statement by specifying the things that are in the world. The word "all" is in the singular number, and this presents collectively what is referred to, indicating that the three things which follow are looked upon as a whole.

the lust of the flesh,—The word *epithumia* signifies a strong desire. The flesh stands for the carnal nature of fallen man, which uses the body as its instrument (1 John 2: 16). "The flesh" is thus "the seat of sin in man;" cp. 2 Pet. 2: 18.* "The lust of the flesh" stands, therefore, for the temptation which proceeds from our corrupt nature, a nature which, owing to sin, stands opposed to the will and commandments of God.

the lust of the eyes,—What has preceded points to temptations from within, this phrase to temptations from without. The eyes are the chief means of communication between external things and the flesh.

The lust of the eyes, then, is a special form of physical gratification. The desire may be for the artistic and æsthetic which, though in itself is beautiful, may so engage the heart as to hinder fellowship with God. Even such things are used by the world so as to exclude God from their thoughts. The believer learns to say, "Turn away mine eyes from beholding vanity."

* For a list of the meanings of *sarx*, "flesh", see *An Expository Dictionary of New Testament Works*, by the writer (Oliphants).

and the vainglory of life,—The word rendered "vainglory" is used elsewhere in the New Testament only in James 4: 16, and there in the plural, "vauntings." It signifies either empty display, or haughty reliance on one's own resources.

Life (*bios*) here signifies the period of human life, as distinct from *zoē*, the vital principle. "The vainglory of life", therefore, is that ostentatious pride which characterizes the present life of the world in its alienation from God.

is not of the Father, but of the world.—That is to say, these things do not spring from the Father nor have they any connection with Him, but find their source in the world, and its spiritual ruler (cp. John 8: 44). The three evils mentioned were the elements in Satan's temptation both of Eve (Gen. 3) and of our Lord (Luke 4).

VERSE 17. **And the world passeth away, and the lust thereof:**— Lit., "is passing away", a continued process (cp. 1 Cor. 7: 31). With regard to whatever time the world of humanity may be viewed, it is transient in character, together with all the evils that characterize it. (See Psa. 39: 6; 103: 15, 16; and James 4: 14.)

but he that doeth the will of God abideth for ever.—Doing the will of God expresses the normal conditions and activity of the believer. The will of God is set in contrast to all that is in the world, for the world lies in the Evil One. Again, doing the will of God is set in contrast to the love of the world; there is a double antithesis. The one who loves the world and walks in its ways passes away with it. On the contrary, love to God involves obedience to His will, and, more than this, whoever does His will is inseparably related to Him; "for whosoever shall do the will of My Father which is in heaven", said the Lord, "he is my brother, and sister, and mother (Matt. 12: 50). There is no "passing away", in the sense of the text, for the believer.

Although the phrase rendered "for ever" is literally "unto the age," the literal rendering does not express the idiom of the original. "For ever" is the accurate equivalent.

VERSE 18. **Little children,**—This begins the second address to the third branch of the heavenly family.

it is the last hour:—The absence of the definite article in the original does not justify the rendering "a last hour." The subject was definite in the minds of both writer and readers. Only one last hour was in view, namely, the closing period previous to the return of the

Lord Jesus. There is a connection of thought between this statement and that of the preceding verse, that "the world passeth away and the lust thereof." "Hour" suggests the brevity and the critical character of the time.

and as ye heard that antichrist cometh,—The term "antichrist" is used in the New Testament only by John, and only in this and the next Epistle; it signifies not only one who takes the place of Christ, but one who is antagonistic to Him. The Antichrist will both seek to usurp the authority of Christ and oppose Him, as did the already existent antichrists by their false teachings (v. 22), cp. 2 Thess. 2: 3.

even now have there arisen many antichrists; whereby we know that it is the last hour.—This the Lord foretold, Matt. 24: 5, 24, cp. Acts 20: 29; 2 Tim. 3: 1; 2 Pet. 2: 1. Contrast with "arisen" (lit., "have become") what was said in 1: 1, as to the eternal pre-existence of Christ. These "antichrists" are evidently precursors of the Antichrist, in whom they will find their climax. The close of this age is, then, to be characterized by antagonism to Christ.

VERSE 19. **They went out from us, but they were not of us;**— While v. 18 draws attention to the existence of the "many antichrists", v. 19 speaks of their connection with the churches. They had evidently sought to identify themselves with the saints. They were not actually united to Christ as real members of His body; professing identification with the saints they partook of their spiritual privileges, but in reality they were traitors to truth, as their false teachings showed.

for if they had been of us, they would have continued with us:— Their dissociation from the believers revealed their lack of real spiritual union with them. The italicized words "no doubt", in the Authorized Version, do not represent anything in the original; they rather weaken the force of what the Apostle wrote. The preposition *meta,* "with", implies not merely that they would have had company with (*sun*) the believers, but that they would have had actual fellowship with them.

but they went out, that they might be made manifest how that they all are not of us.—Here the elliptical character of the original necessitates the insertion of some phrase like "they went out", or "this they did," or "this happened." What our English versions have is satisfactory. The R.V. rendering "they all are not of us" is necessary to a right understanding of the meaning. It lays due stress upon the fact that not one of these teachers was actually possessed of spiritual life and enjoyed true fellowship with the saints. The Apostle is not making a selection, as if some of them were real and others false, as the A.V. suggests. The necessary separation of the "not" from the "all" makes the negation of universal application. Cp. the original of Matt. 24: 22, and contrast 1 Cor. 15: 39.

It was according to the Divine purpose that these teachers should be manifested in their true character, as not belonging to the family of God. The Apostle is not teaching here that a Christian cannot fall away and backslide. That is not the subject with which he is now dealing. He is making clear the distinction between the genuine and the false in matters of doctrine, as he does in the next chapter in regard to matters of practice.

VERSE 20.   **And ye have an anointing from the Holy One,—**"And" is the rendering of the Greek *kai*, not "but" (as in the A.V.). The Apostle is simply putting two contrasting subjects side by side. There are the future Antichrist and the present antichrist on the one hand, and the true Christ and the children of God on the other. There is no need to render by "but" in order to show the contrast. That is sufficiently brought out by the emphatic pronoun "ye", which requires due stress on the part of one who is reading aloud.

The "anointing" (*chrisma*), preferable to the rendering "unction," signifies that which is carried out by the act of anointing, and thus stands here for the effect of the act itself, the impartation of the Holy Spirit, who was symbolically set forth by the material oil with which the act was carried out in the former age in the nation of Israel in the case of kings, priests and prophets. For the figurative use of the anointing see, *e.g.*, Is. 61: 1; Acts 10: 38; 2 Cor. 1: 21, 22. The word *chrisma* is found only here and in v. 27 in the New Testament.

While Christ Himself was anointed by the Holy Spirit in the days of His flesh (Acts 10: 38), here He, as the Holy One, is the Anointer. For the title "Holy One" see Psa. 16: 10. For the anointing of the priests in the nation of Israel see Ex. 29: 7, 21; Lev. 8: 30. All believers are priests unto God (1 Pet. 5: 9; Rev. 1: 6). They become so, not by attainment, but in virtue of the gift of the Holy Spirit, who is received at the new birth, and from that time indwells the believer. The gift of the Holy Spirit is not contingent upon maturity in the Christian life, nor upon degree of spiritual attainment. Upon believing we are sealed with the Holy Spirit (Eph. 1: 13, where the R.V. rightly has "having also believed, ye were sealed"; there is no "after" in the original, as in the A.V.). The Holy Spirit indwelling the believer is His Guide "into all the truth" (John 16:13), and this has an important bearing upon the present passage.

and ye know all things.—Even the babes in Christ have the power of the Holy Spirit given to them in order that they may know the truth and disown what is opposed to it. There is much to be said for the marginal reading of the R.V., "and ye all know," in which case the beginning of v. 21 is parenthetic and the statement is resumed in the words "ye know it" (the truth). But in any case the meaning is much the same as in the text, for what the Apostle is pointing out is, that it is his readers, and not the false and antichristian teachers, who possess the true knowledge, and that it is possessed in virtue of the anointing, which the false teachers lack.

The believer is therefore not justified in praying for the anointing, for that is his by reason of his regenerate condition. He may pray that the power of the Spirit may be experienced, and that he may be filled with the Spirit, but to ask for the gift that has already been imparted indicates a lack of the apprehension of the goodness and grace of God in having bestowed it.

VERSE 21. **I have not written unto you because ye know not the truth, but because ye know it, and because no lie is of the truth.**—The opening words of this verse are probably to be rendered in the present tense, which corresponds to the epistolary past tense of the original, the writer looking on, as was customary, to the time when his letter would reach his readers; in that case the rendering should be "I am not writing unto you because, etc." The Apostle is not suggesting that his readers are ignorant of the truth, but rather that, considering that they actually possess it, they are thereby enabled to distinguish between truth and error.

The truth springs from God "who cannot lie" (Tit. 1: 2): lying springs from the Devil (John 8: 44). There is no neutral ground between truth and error, just as, as the Apostle has pointed out, there is no neutral ground between the mere professor and the actual possessor. Truth is truth, and error is error. Their source and their practice are entirely removed one from the other.

VERSE 22. **Who is the liar but he that denieth that Jesus is the Christ ?**—The definite article does not point to any particular person. The Apostle passes, from the abstract in v. 21, to the concrete, and the article marks anyone as representatively the liar, who denies that Jesus is the Christ. The denial that Jesus is the Christ is the representative falsehood.

The phrase "he that denieth" is, literally, "the one denying," suggesting a habitual denial. The phrase, which consists of the article with the present participle, is virtually a noun, "the denier"; such a representative person was Cerinthus, whose Gnostic teachings have been mentioned in the Introduction.

This is the antichrist, even he that denieth the Father and the Son.— The definite article here has a generalizing, or representative, force. While the great future Antichrist is in view, he is not the single person particularized. Just as with "the liar," in the earlier part of the verse, so any teacher who denies the Father and the Son is a representative of the sort of person that the Antichrist will be.

While a change is made from the denial that Jesus is the Christ to the denial of the Father and the Son, yet there is not a great difference; the denial of the former truth involves the denial of the Persons. The relation of the Son to the Father, and their essential and eternal unity, are alike comprehended in the truth that Jesus is the Christ. To confess the latter is at once to confess the truth of His eternal Sonship in relation to the Father. Father is a relative term. Fatherhood involves sonship, and the Son, who is also the Christ, is the revelation of the Father. Apart from Him the Father cannot be known (Matt. 11: 27).

VERSE 23. **Whosoever denieth the Son, the same hath not the Father: he that confesseth the Son hath the Father also.**—This confirms the preceding statement and is an emphatic expansion of it, negatively and positively. A closer rendering of the original would be "Whosoever denieth the Son hath not even the Father." More is taught here than the essential unity between the Father and the Son. It is true that to deny the One is to deny the Other, but, more than this, to deny the Son is to deprive oneself of relationship to, and communion with, the Father. Professed acknowledgment is one thing, actual possession is another. Apart from the latter mere profession is meaningless and does not receive Divine recognition. Again, not only does confession of the Son, that is, confession that Jesus is the Christ and all that is involved therein, carry with it the confession of the Father, it involves, too, Divine relationship and communion with the Father. That is more than holding an article of faith or knowing the will of the Father. Confession of Christ goes with possession of Christ, and those who receive Him become children of God (John 1: 12). To acknowledge the Fatherhood of God and deny the Deity of Christ is utterly incompatible. For the association of the truth that Jesus is the Christ, with that of His relationship with the Father see Peter's confession (Matt. 16: 16).

Although the latter part of this verse is put in italics in the A.V. the weight of MS. evidence shows that it is an essential part of the original. That which is contained in the confession is likewise set forth in the Lord's discourse to the Pharisees in the 8th chapter of the Gospel, vv. 16 to 55, and should be read in connection with it.

VERSE 24. **As for you,**—With great emphasis upon the "you"; the Apostle is still addressing the young converts.

let that abide in you which ye heard from the beginning.—Note the difference of the order here from that in 1: 1, "That which was from the beginning, that which we have heard." Their hearing the truth from the beginning, that is, when the testimony was first given to them, was one thing; that the Person who formed the subject of the testimony was "from the beginning," pre-existent, unoriginated, was another.

That the phrase, "let that abide in you" comes first indicates that it bears special stress, suggesting their need of steadfastness in the truth which they had received.

If that which ye heard from the beginning abide in you, ye also shall abide in the Son, and in the Father.—As Christ the Son of God is the Truth, and as the Word of God which is taught is the truth, to abide in the truth is to abide in Him who is the Son of the Father, and therefore in the Father too, for the Son and the Father are one. Note the reverse order of Persons from that in verse 22. There it was "the Father and the Son"; here it is "the Son and the Father." As Westcott says, "Here the thought is that of rising through the confession of the Son to the knowledge of the Father; there the thought is of the issue of denial culminating in the denial of the Father."

The subject of this passage may be put under three headings:

(1) Denying the Father and the Son (v. 22),
(2) Confessing the Son and the Father (v. 23),
(3) Abiding in the Son and in the Father (v. 24).

VERSE 25. **And this is the promise which He promised us, even the life eternal.**—While the pronoun "this" points to what follows, as in other places in the Epistle (see 1: 5; 3: 23, *e.g.*), yet there is a close connection with the preceeding statements. It may be perhaps expressed thus: "Those who confess the Son and the Father, and who give evidence of their relationship with Them by abiding in the truth, these are they who realize that they have eternal life, according to the Divine promise." There is a stress on the word "He", and the Promiser in Christ.

In this verse the distinction is continued between the true child of God, the actual possessor of life, and the false teachers, the deniers of Christ, who though identifying themselves with the converts were themselves void of life. See also the next verse.

VERSE 26. **These things have I written unto you concerning them who would lead you astray.**—"These things" would seem to point to what is contained in verses 18-25. The participial construction, rendered "they that would lead you astray," is practically a noun, "your deceivers." The true character of the false teachers is, then, to be discerned.

VERSE 27. **And as for you,**—The connecting word *kai* cannot mean "but," as in the A.V. That rendering was adopted in order to express a contrast; while the contrast is there it does not justify a mistranslation. The contrast is sufficiently brought out by "as for you." By the "And" the Apostle puts the false and the true side by side, not that they may be grouped together, but by way of continuing his appeal to the readers in view of their danger.

the anointing which ye received of Him abideth in you,—For the subject of the anointing see notes on verse 20. The word "of" represents the preposition *apo*, which signifies "from" and suggests the Divine source of the anointing. The Apostle more frequently uses *para* with this verb, which thus means "to receive at the hand of" (see John 5: 41, 44; 2 John 4; Rev. 2: 27). As the anointing symbolically stands for the Holy Spirit, it is clear from this statement that even in the youngest believer the Spirit of God dwells.

and ye need not that anyone teach you;—This does not suggest that they were without the need of teaching, but rather that with the Divine power given to them to detect false teachers they were able to refuse their teachings. The ascended Lord has given spiritual gifts in the Church, apostles, prophets, evangelists, pastors, teachers, and these are for the building up of the Body of Christ (Eph. 4: 11, 12); but the Apostle's point here is that believers are able by the Spirit's power to be secure against all deceits of the enemy. Human instrumentality was never intended to take the place of dependence upon God; yet, on the other hand, young believers are to be free from that fanaticism which refuses the help of spiritual gifts in the Church.

but as His anointing teacheth you concerning all things, and is true, and is no lie, and even as it taught you, ye abide in Him.—That the anointing, or the Holy Spirit, teaches us concerning all things, confirms, in a positive way, what has just been put negatively. Again, the Holy Spirit is the "Spirit of truth" (John 14: 17; 15: 26; 16: 13); for that reason the anointing is true.

That the anointing "is no lie" is not a mere repetition of the statement that it is true. It sets in more vivid contrast the falsehoods of the errorists. They are not mere promulgators of speculative theories, they are liars (see verse 22); they are directly antagonistic to the truth. On the contrary, an essential feature of the anointing is the impartation of truth. The effect of the work of the Spirit is consistent with His character; He imparts truth because He is true.

The word rendered "ye abide" may be either indicative, as in the text, or imperative, "abide ye", as in the R.V. margin. If the former is the meaning, then we may understand the argument somewhat as follows: "the special subject about which I am writing concerns those who are deceiving you; but as to you, since the anointing you have received abides in you, you need no such teaching. You have a Divine Teacher, to whom listening, you abide in Him." If the imperative mood is to be understood the meaning is practically the same.

A brief outline of the Epistle thus far, under four headings, may be useful:—

(1) Chapter 1: 1–7 shows to what infinite blessings believers have been called.
(2) They have, however, many dangers within and without. There is firstly, their own sin (1: 8; 2: 1); but God has provided a remedy for that (2: 2–6).
(3) There is a world of darkness around them, but God has provided light, and power to overcome (2: 7–17).
(4) Finally, there are false teachers, but God has given the indwelling Spirit to provide against them (2: 18–27).

(C)   Verse 28

(Resuming 2:12)

1. The command—"abide in Him",

2. The reasons for the command:
   (a) positive—boldness in His Parousia,
   (b) negative—absence of shame in His Parousia.

VERSE 28. **And now, my little children, abide in Him;**—As mentioned previously, the word *teknia*, rendered "little children", is the same as in verse 12, whereas *paidia* is the word in verses 13 and 18, representing the three branches of the heavenly family. Having finished his special address to the fathers, the young men and the little children, the Apostle now resumes his address to the whole family, taking up the thought he has just expressed in verse 27 of abiding in Christ, and giving it as a command to all.

that, if He shall be manifested, we may have boldness, and not be ashamed before Him at His coming.—The introduction of this subject by the word "if" does not imply any doubt as to Christ's return. It simply marks the time as unfixed and as possible of occurrence within the lifetime of his readers. The change to "when", as in the A.V., seems to have been made in order to avoid the suggestion of a doubt, but there was no need of this.

The manifestation spoken of here is to believers only, at the time of the Rapture (1 Thess. 4), and not to the world. The world *phaneroō*, "to manifest," has various applications with reference to Christ. It is used of His Incarnation (1 Tim. 3: 16; 1 John 1: 2). It is also used of His appearance after His resurrection when He manifested Himself to His disciples only (John 21: 1, 14). In Col. 3: 4, it refers to His manifestation with all His saints to the world when He comes with them in glory for the overthrow of His foes and the setting up of His Kingdom. The context in each passage guides us as to the application. Here the reference is to the circumstances at the Judgment-seat of Christ, before which believers, and only believers, are all to be made manifest, "that each one may receive the things done in the body" (2 Cor. 5: 10). That this is the time referred to is indicated by the words "that . . . we may have boldness." The "we" includes both the Apostle and his readers, both the pastor and those for whom he has cared spiritually. Anticipating the time of the Judgment-seat he looks forward to see in them then the fruit of his labours on their behalf, so that he and they too may receive a full reward as a result of their abiding in Christ. The boldness which he trusts will characterize both him and them in that august scene is set in contrast to the shame which would result from their having failed to abide in Christ in this life, and their consequent loss of reward at the Judgment-seat.

The word rendered "before" is *apo*, which ordinarily means "from" (see margin). But the literal sense is not to be pressed, as if the meaning intended was that saints will shrink back from the presence of the Lord. The rendering "before" is adequate. There is no intimation whatever here that some believers will be left behind on earth at the time of the Rapture through their failure in the matter of watchfulness. What is referred to in the phrase "at His coming" is not simply the occurrence of the Rapture itself but the period and circumstances which follow.

The word "Parousia" rendered "coming" literally denotes "presence." It is a noun formed from the verb *pareimi*, to be present, and thus signifies "a being present with." In Phil. 2: 12, Paul uses the word in the phrase "not as in my presence only" (it could not be rendered "coming" there) and contrasts it with his absence from Philippi. The translation "coming" is misleading. There are other words which denote "coming", such as *eleusis* (Acts 7: 52), and *eisodos* (13: 24), and the corresponding verb *erchomai* (Luke 12: 45, etc.). Whereas these words fix the attention on the journey to and the arrival at a place, *parousia* fixes it on the stay which follows on the arrival there. It would be preferable therefore to transliterate the word rather than translate it, that is, to use *parousia* rather than 'coming' wherever the reference is to the Lord Jesus. Where *parousia* is used of the Lord Jesus it refers to a defined period. Thus in 2 Pet. 1: 16 it describes, not the daily and general companying of the Lord with His disciples among the people, but that limited period during which He was transfigured before them (Matt. 17: 1–8). Where it is used prophetically, *parousia* refers to a period beginning with the descent of the Lord from Heaven into the air (1 Thess. 4: 16, 17) and ending with His revelation and manifestation to the world.

During the Parousia of the Lord in the air with His people, Paul expected to give account of his stewardship before the Judgment-seat of Christ (1 Cor. 4: 1–5; 2 Cor. 5: 10); the presence there of the Thessalonian converts and their commendation by the Lord, would mean reward to the evangelists who had been the means of their conversion, and to the pastors and teachers who had laboured among them.

The Parousia of the Lord Jesus is thus a period with a beginning, a course, and a conclusion. The beginning is prominent in 1 Thess. 4: 15; 5: 23; 2 Thess. 2: 1; 1 Cor. 15: 23; James 5: 7, 2 Pet. 3: 4; the course, here and in 1 Thess. 2: 19 and 3: 13; Matt. 24: 3, 37, 39; the conclusion, in 2 Thess. 2: 8; Matt. 24: 27.

CHAPTER III

Analysis of Chapter 2: 29—3: 24

	Chapter—Verses
(1) The family characteristic:	2: 29—3: 1

(a) The character of the Father—righteousness 2: 29a
(b) The character of the children—the practice of righteousness 2: 29b
(c) The Divine relationship: 3: 1

    1. An evidence of the Father's love . . . "behold"
    2. The character of the love . . . "what manner . . ."
    3. The mode of the bestowal . . . "called children of God"
    4. The relationship emphasized (R.V.) . . . "and such we are"
    5. The consequence . . . "Therefore . . ."

(2) The family hope and its effect: 3: 2, 3

(a) The present fact of the relationship 2a
(b) The unrevealed prospect, "what we shall be" 2b
(c) The revealed prospect, likeness to Christ: 2c
    The time, the season
(d) The present effect: 3

    1. The direction of the hope—"set on Him,"
    2. The purifying power of the hope—"purifieth himself,"
    3. The standard of hope—"even as He is pure."

(3) The heavenly family and the opposite one: 3: 4–12

(a) Sin and its practice: 4
    1. The practice characterized
    2. Sin characterized
(b) Christ and sin: 5
    1. Its removal, the purpose of His manifestation
    2. His own sinlessness

The close of the second chapter is really introductory to the third. Here the Apostle passes from the subject of light to that of love, which forms the keyword of this central portion of the Epistle as far as chapter 5: 5. While righteousness is the initial theme, as a characteristic of the heavenly family, it finds its evidence in brotherly love, and in this respect the children of God are intended to stand out in marked contrast to the world (see 3: 10, *e.g.*).

Chapters 2: 29—3: 1

VERSE 29. **If ye know that He is righteous,**—The preceding verse speaks of Christ. The word rendered "know" (*oida*) signifies intuitive knowledge, knowledge simply possessed. Righteousness, the condition of being right, is marked as an essential characteristic of God.

ye know—This represents a different word, *ginōskō*, which signifies knowledge gained by experience. The change from the word in the first part of the verse may be brought out as follows: "If ye are aware that He is righteous ye recognize by experience that etc." For further contrasts *oida* is the word in 2: 11, 20, 21, whereas *ginōskō* is the word in 2: 3, 4, 5, 13, 14, 18. Cp. *oida* and *ginōskō* in that order in John 13: 7; 21:17, and in the opposite order in 14: 7.

that everyone also that doeth righteousness is begotten of Him.— The word "also" marks emphatically the identification, in the matter of righteousness, of the children of God with their Heavenly Father. The word rendered "doeth" is in the present continuous tense and marks the doing of righteousness as a habit. Moreover, the present participle of the verb is used together with the definite article, and this virtually constitutes a noun. Literally the phrase is "everyone the one doing righteousness", *i.e.*, "every doer of righteousness", that is to say, he who habitually practises righteousness. It is this which gives evidence of Divine sonship.

In the preceding verse it is Christ who has been mentioned. In this verse the phrase "begotten of Him" points to God the Father. The Apostle lays stress on the truth that Christ and the Father are one, and that Christ is God revealed to man; hence he makes the contrast from one to another almost imperceptible. "When John thinks of God in relation to men, he never thinks of Him apart from Christ (see 1 John 5: 20), and, again, he never thinks of Christ in His human nature without adding the thought of His Divine nature. Thus a rapid transition is possible from the one aspect of the Lord's Divine human Person to the other" (Westcott).

Righteousness is a quality said of both God the Father and of Christ; of God in 1 John 1: 9; John 17: 25; Rev. 16: 5, and of Christ in 1 John 2: 1, and 4: 7. Everyone then who is a doer of righteousness has been begotten of Him, for he manifests, as a characteristic of his life, that he is possessed of the same character as the One who begat him. This is the first occurrence of this phrase "begotten of God" in this Epistle.

Chapter 3

VERSE 1.   **Behold, what manner of love,**—The word "Behold" is in the plural. It is not an exclamation but a command to all believers. The word *potapos*, "what-manner-of," always indicates astonishment and usually admiration also (see Matt. 8: 27; Mark 13: 1; Luke 1: 29; 7: 39; 2 Pet. 3: 11). The subject of Divine love is here introduced in the Epistle, following the subject of light.

the Father hath bestowed upon us,—The order of the words in the original lays stress upon "the Father," though stress is not absent from the "hath bestowed" and "us"; each word is intended to arrest the attention. Love is represented as a gift, or bestowment, here only in the New Testament. The Father is spoken of, not merely because the title "God" would be unsuitable in view of the phrase that follows, "the children of God", but rather as being in keeping with the theme and circumstances of the heavenly family and its relationships.

that we should be called—While the conjunction "that" introduces the point in which the love is expressed, it also suggests the Divine purpose in bestowing it. The Apostle speaks of the relationship as a calling, rather than saying that we have become children of God; he thus suggests the dignity of the relationship.

the children of God:—The absence of the article throws stress upon the relationship involved. *Tekna* is the word rendered "children," not *huioi*, "sons." The Apostle never speaks of believers as sons of God, but always as children. The title "Son" is reserved in his writings for the Son of God. Paul speaks of believers in both respects, specially stressing their adoption; John stresses the thought of generation.

Again, the absence of the article in the original before the word "God" brings into prominence, not that we are children of One who is Divine and not human, but rather that we are related to One who is our God.

and such we are.—Literally "and we are." By this addition, which is in keeping with the Apostle's style, he confirms the relationship, as if to arrest the thought of the reader with the marvel of the way in which Divine love has been exercised.

For this cause—At first sight this might appear to refer to the sentence that follows, but in John's writings it is usual for this phrase, not merely to anticipate what follows, but also to refer back to what precedes. The phrase thus connects the two; what follows explains the sequence of the central statement from what precedes. In this instance we might put the connection as follows—"We are children of God, and because of this the world knows us not, for it knew Him not." For further illustrations of such connection see John 5: 16; 5: 18; 8: 47; 10: 17; 12: 39.

the world knoweth us not, because it knew Him not.—The verb rendered "knoweth" and "knew" is *ginōskō* which suggests that the world has not even begun to gain by experience a knowledge of the children of God. Cp. John 15: 19, in regard to God's children and 8: 19, in regard to the Son of God; there the word is *oida*, signifying intuitive knowledge.

VERSE 2. **Beloved,**—This term has been used once in the Epistle previously, at 2: 7, R.V., and there because the Apostle was about to make reference to the subject of brotherly love (2: 9–11); in the central part of the Epistle where "love" is the main subject, the title occurs very frequently.

now are we children of God,—This resumes and emphasises the already mentioned fact. The "now" is set in contrast to the future. That we are children suggests that, blessed as the relationship is, this is not the final state, and though the Apostle does not definitely mention the maturity of sonship, yet what he is now about to state implies it.

and it is not yet made manifest what we shall be.—"Not yet" is set in contrast to "now." Instead of the A.V. "appear," the R.V. rightly renders by the passive voice "made manifest," which more definitely indicates that this is to be the act of God. That we are now children of God is a foretaste of what we are going to be. The present state is the guarantee of future glories.

We know—There is no "but" in the original in the best manuscripts. What is now to be stated is not mentioned by way of contrast to the fact that it is not yet made manifest what we shall be, it rather states an assurance in addition to what we are already. "We know" translates the verb *oida* in contrast to the word *ginōskō*; it is not a matter of progress in experience but of absolute certainty intuitively realized.

that, if He shall be manifested,—The "if" does not suggest any doubt about the fact of Christ's being manifested, it directs the attention to the effects of the manifestation rather than the time. As further illustrations of this use of the conjunction "if", not to imply supposition but to stress the fact conveyed by the statement that follows, see the Lord's words "I, if I be lifted up from the earth" (Jn. 12: 32), and "If I go and prepare a place for you" (14: 3).

A possible alternative rendering is "If it shall be manifested" that is to say, "if what we shall be shall be manifested," but the subsequent context confirms the R.V. text.

we shall be like Him; for we shall see Him even as He is.—Our future likeness to Christ is the dominant fact in the passage so far. God made man in His own image (Gen. 1: 26, 27). The likeness was marred at the Fall. It is to be renewed by Christ when He is manifested and to be renewed in the greater glory of resurrection (Phil. 3: 21), and that on the ground of His atoning sacrifice and His resurrection.

In this life men become like the objects of their worship. As to idols, they that make them shall be like unto them (Ps. 115: 8). As to believers, even now, "reflecting as a mirror the glory of the Lord" they are "transfigured into the same image from glory to glory" (2 Cor. 3: 18). What is now a process will be instantaneously an accomplished fact when He, whom we now see and worship by faith, comes again and receives us to Himself, according to His promise.

The "even as" stresses the fullness of the fact. We shall see Him no longer darkly in a mirror but "face to face." That is what will take place at the Rapture (1 Thess. 4: 13–17), and the statement shows that the manifestation spoken of in this verse will take place at the time of the Rapture rather than at the Second Advent, when He will be manifested with all His saints to the world.

VERSE 3. **And everyone that hath this hope**—This, which is a participial phrase in the original, does not describe a certain number of believers who are characterized in this way in distinction from other believers, it lays down what is a normal characteristic, common to all the children of God.

set on Him—The hope is not described as being in the believer, as the A.V. suggests (it cannot be otherwise than in a person himself). It is a hope set on Christ, a hope that rests upon Him. For the same preposition *epi* with the verb to hope, and with reference to the hope as set on God, see Rom. 15: 12; 1 Tim. 4: 10. This is the only reference to hope in John's Epistles.

purifieth himself,—While the verb *hagnizō* is sometimes used, both in the LXX and the New Testament, of ceremonial purification, here it is used with a moral significance. The purification is from everything that is inconsistent with the character and will of the Lord. This truth is directed against the Gnostic teaching that sin does not pollute the enlightened person. The tense is the continuous present and thus indicates the habit of resisting every defiling influence and keeping oneself free from it. Compare and contrast 1: 7, where cleansing from sin that has been committed is bestowed on the ground of the blood of Christ.

even as He is pure.—In this verse again, though the Apostle has been referring to God the Father, yet he passes characteristically, without direct indication, to the Person of Christ, and is speaking here of His moral perfections as manifested in the days of His flesh. The word *hagnos* betokens the purity of one who, having been subjected to temptation, overcomes it. This is true of Christ, and His pureness is the standard set for the believer. The Apostle does not say that, "He purified Himself", but that "He is pure." It is the believer who has to purify himself. What was an inherent quality in Him is a quality which the believer is to set before himself as an attainment. See Heb. 12: 4.

VERSE 4. **Every one that doeth sin**—Here again, the tense is the present continuous and expresses a practice and not an act. The A.V. "committeth" is misleading. Neither here nor anywhere in this passage is the committal of an act in view. The Apostle is dealing with that which characterizes the life. The purpose is to contrast the children of God with those who are not (see verse 10). It would be well always to avoid the use of the verb "commit" in this passage. In the original the contrast is clearly marked between this phrase and that in

2: 29, "every one that doeth righteousness" (see note there). As righteousness was there marked as a characteristic of one who was born of God, so here the opposite is expressed.

doeth also lawlessness:—Again the A.V. "transgresseth the law" is misleading, as suggesting an act. The parallelism between the phrases should be maintained. The order in the original is chiasmic, or crosswise—verb, noun, noun, verb—"every one doing sin, lawlessness also doeth." John's use of the present tense of the verb *poieō*, "to do", expresses the meaning of the alternative verb *prassō*, "to practise." The manner of life which is marked by continuing to do sin is described by the phrase "doeth lawlessness," which is constant disregard of the Law of God. As, then, doing righteousness is an evidence of the new birth, so doing lawlessness is an evidence of not being born of God.

and sin is lawlessness.—Sin and lawlessness are different aspects of the same thing. A section of the Gnostic teachers taught that a certain attainment of knowledge placed a person above moral law, in which case one was rendered neither better for keeping it nor worse for breaking it. The teaching of this passage therefore strikes a blow against such error. The practice of sin is shown to be entirely incompatible with being a child of God.

VERSE 5. **And ye know—Oidate,** "ye know as a fact essential to the Christian faith." The Apostle's constant appeal to the knowledge possessed by believers is a set-off against the knowledge in which the Gnostics boasted.

that He was manifested—This, which refers to Christ's Incarnation, assumes His pre-existence. From the glory where He had been with the Father He came to earth becoming Incarnate, and so manifested to men. This the Lord speaks of as His mission from the Father John 5: 37; 8: 18, where the verb is *pempō*, "to send," and cp. 4: 34; 6: 38). He also speaks of it as a sending involving a commission (see John 3: 17; 10: 36, where the word is *apostellō* as also in 1 John 4: 10). His coming is spoken of again simply as an historical event (see John 1: 11; 8: 42) and as that which has had abiding effects (see John 3: 19; 8: 14; 1 John 5: 20).

to take away sins;—*Airō*, means "to remove by lifting," cp. 1 Pet. 2:24, "Who His own self bear our sins in His body upon the tree"—

not "unto" but "upon." The point in the present passage, however, is not the mode in which Christ took away sins but the fact that His having become Incarnate in order to take them away shows that sin is incompatible with the Divine relationship of being children of God; in other words, not the nature of the atonement is here in view but the effect of it in the life.

and in Him is no sin.—Lit., "and in Him sin is not." He is essentially and eternally the sinless One, and this has been proved in the days of His flesh. This statement is not put as what believers know in addition to the preceding fact, though that is so; rather it is a truth independently expressed, and by it the Apostle confirms his argument that sin is incompatible with relationship with God. The members of the heavenly family, so far from continuing in sin, as before they became children of God, are united to One who Himself both was the Bearer of sins and is essentially sinless. There is this, also, that the approved sinlessness of Christ showed that He, and He alone, was fit and competent to take away sins.

The way in which the writers of the New Testament state the sinlessness of Christ is appropriate respectively to their characteristics. Peter, the man of action, says, "He did no sin" (1 Pet. 2: 22); Paul, the man of knowledge, says, "He knew no sin" (2 Cor. 5: 21); John, the man of intimate personal acquaintance with Christ in the days of His flesh, says, "In Him is no sin." Thus completely does the Spirit of God safeguard, in the testimony of the New Testament, the character of Christ.

VERSE 6. **Whosoever abideth in Him sinneth not:**—The "whosoever" represents the same phrase in the original as "every one" in 2: 29; 3: 3, and 3: 4, R.V. Both verbs "abideth" and "sinneth" are in the present continuous tense and express the normal state. Abiding in Christ and continuance in sin are incongruous. It is true that even an act of sin is inconsistent with abiding in Christ, but, as elsewhere in this passage, the Apostle is dealing with characteristics and habits, and not acts. He spoke of acts of sin in 1: 8–10. To abide in Christ involves the habit of communion with God and the habitual fulfilment of His will. This passage is not to be explained by Rom. 7: 20. Paul is there dealing with another aspect of truth.

whosoever sinneth hath not seen Him, neither knoweth Him.—This alone is sufficient to make clear that practice is in view, and not the committal of an act. Every believer does sin, see 1: 8. Yet the believer is one who has seen Christ, by faith, and knows Him. What is implied here, then, is a ruling principle of the life. He who, being a believer, has seen Christ and knows Him, does not continue in sin. Possibly the Apostle is making an allusion to some who claimed a certain measure of superiority because of having seen Christ in the flesh. The sight to which he refers, however, is the spiritual sight of faith, the faith which appropriates Him by spiritual experience and produces the consciousness of His presence, and so imparts a knowledge of Him. To know Him is to acknowledge and appreciate His character and to live in the practical enjoyment of relationship to Him.

We might have expected, by way of contrast to the preceding statement, "every one that sinneth abideth not in Him", but the Apostle's manner in expressing antitheses is to strengthen and extend the thought of the preceding statement.

VERSE 7. **My little children,**—The reiteration of this mode of address now carries with it a note of tender solemnity. The Apostle is reaching the height of this part of his subject.

let no man lead you astray:—The warning enforces the gravity of the error with which he is dealing, namely, that it is possible, though living in sin, to have spiritual life, and that as long as a man believes himself to be spiritual he is above contamination. The verb, *planeō*, to lead astray, is the same as in 1:8.

he that doeth righteousness is righteous, even as He is righteous:—That is to say, "he who does righteousness habitually." To fulfil righteousness in its completeness, as a manner of life, is evidence of identification with "Jesus Christ the righteous." No matter how much one may claim to have a knowledge of Divine truth, it goes for nothing unless the life is in accordance with the truth, and therefore with the character and walk of Him who Himself was and is the Truth. The "He" in the last clause of the verse is Christ, and in the original the pronoun used carries emphasis. The Epistle of James stresses the deadness of faith without works, John's Epistle the deadness of knowledge without works. For the subject of doing righteousness see 2:29.

VERSE 8. **he that doeth sin is of the Devil;**—For the phrase "he that doeth sin," as set in contrast to the doing of righteousness see verse 4. Again, the Apostle does not give the exact contrasting parallel with what he has just stated, which would have been "he that doeth sin is unrighteous even as the Devil is unrighteous." He goes further and expresses definitely the evil spiritual relationship, in contrast to the Divine relationship of his readers. Not that the Devil is the source of anyone's existence, for, as Augustine says, "The Devil made no man, begat no man, created no man." The Devil is the source of sin, and therefore the one who leads a sinful life is spiritually connected with him. Not that man is helpless in his continuance of evil, as if he were void of responsibility in the matter, but that, inasmuch as the habit of his life is the same as that which characterizes the Devil, a spiritual relationship exists between them.

for the Devil sinneth from the beginning.—There is stress upon the phrase "from the beginning." Sin began when Satan first sinned. The use of the present tense in the statement, instead of the past "has sinned," marks the fact that he himself is sinful and his course is unceasingly one of sin. By his misrepresentation of God, which is implied in the title "Devil", he has ever sought to attack the soul of man, endeavouring to instil reasons for doubt and distrust of God. That is the evidence of Scripture from the first to the last, cp. John 8: 44.

To this end was the Son of God manifested, that He might destroy the works of the Devil.—The full title, "the Son of God," is mentioned here for the first time in this Epistle. Previously He has been spoken of as "the Son." While, in this Epistle, as the Son He is made to stand out distinctly from the children of God, here in the full title He also stands out as the One who, being possessed of essential, un-originated relationship with the Father, came forth from the Father and came into the world in order to destroy the works of God's opponent. Further, in the mention of this title Christ is set in contrast to those who in their deliberate habit of evil doing are spiritual children of the Devil.

While the verb *luō*, to destroy, literally means "to loose," the literal meaning must not be pressed here. The word is used of that method of destruction by which a thing is broken and nullified, and this is the effect of Christ's work on the Cross upon the works of the Devil. These works are the operation of the Evil One upon the human heart, by which man, yielding to his suggestions and influence, has fallen into sin and continues therein.

This verse does not provide ground for the assumption that all mankind will eventually be delivered from the effects of sin. What is stated is the means God has taken, the provision He has made, for the accomplishment of the end in view. The whole tenor of the passage stresses the fact that man by continuing in sin may refuse to avail himself of the effects of the work of Christ. This statement in verse 8 resumes that in verse 5, setting forth the subjects as in connection with God's Adversary, and not merely with sin, and thus preparing the way for the statements of verses 9 and 10.

VERSE 9. **Whosoever is begotten of God doeth no sin,**—This is set in contrast to the beginning of verse 8. The phrase rendered "is begotten" is in the perfect tense, "has been begotten"; in other words, "has become and therefore remains a child of God." The phrase "to be begotten of God" is, in the New Testament, confined to the writings of the Apostle John.

The statement here again conveys the thought of sinning as a practice, a habit. The better and accurate rendering would be "doeth not sin." "Doeth no sin" states what is not a fact, for it suggests that no sin is committed by such. What is here taught is not that the Divine nature in man does not sin, and that it is only the old nature, the flesh, that sins; the fact is that the Apostle is still distinguishing between the child of God and the unregenerate.

because his seed abideth in him:—It is possible to understand this as meaning that one who is a child of God (God's seed) abides in Him. Perhaps, however, the seed signifies the Divine principle of imparted life in the believer, and this, once it is imparted, is unalterable; it remains in the believer. The child of God stands eternally related to Christ. The one who goes on doing sin (in other words, lives in sin), has never become a child of God. He has not the principle of life in Christ in him. There are other interpretations, but this seems to be in accordance with the general tenor of the Epistle and the immediate context, both preceding and succeeding.

and he cannot sin, because he is begotten of God.—Here again, not the committal of an act is in view, but continuance in sin. It is not a case merely of moral impossibility; relationship to God, once it is established, not only abides for ever but precludes the possibility of continuance of sin as a practice of the life. This difference between the children of God and those who are not is categorically stated in the next verse.

VERSE 10. **In this**—While this phrase recalls what has just been said, it also serves to introduce the contrast about to be stated. For in verse 9 the Apostle has mentioned what characterizes the children of God. In verse 10 he is about to restate what characterizes the children of the Devil. "In this" governs what is said of both families.

the children of God are manifest, and the children of the Devil:— The distinction is now clearly marked by the contrasting relationships. The tree is known by its fruit. Whether a person is born of God or is unregenerate is to be tested by his manner of life.

While the phrase "the children of the Devil" does not occur elsewhere in the New Testament, yet the Lord interpreted the tares in the parable, as "the sons of the Evil One", the word "sons" conveying the thought of likeness to parentage. In John 8: 44 the Lord says to the Jews who were intent upon murdering Him, "ye are of your father the Devil, and the lusts of your father it is your will to do." Again, Elymas the sorcerer was called a "son of the Devil" (Acts 13: 10). While the word "children" here expresses relationship, yet the Apostle is stressing the evidence of it rather than the mere relationship.

Whosoever doeth not righteousness is not of God, neither he that loveth not his brother.—Literally, "and he that loveth not." Here the "and" is virtually "even", and introduces what is explanatory of what has preceded. Not to love one's brother is a special form of not doing righteousness, as righteousness, or right-wiseness, is being right with God, and brotherly love is a mark of being right with God; the absence of it is a mark of the absence of Divine relationship. "The whole Law is fulfilled in one word, even in this, Thou shalt love thy neighbour as thyself" (Gal. 5: 14). To fulfil the Law is to be right with God and so to do righteousness. A proof of the existence of Divine relationship, then, consists in the manifestation of love to others. One who is born of God will love those whom God loves.

In this verse the article is absent before "righteousness' whereas it is present in verse 7. While its presence in verse 7 stresses the completeness and unity of righteousness, its absence here stresses the character of righteousness in a special way.

VERSE 11. **For this is the message which ye heard from the beginning, that we should love one another:**—More literally, "Because the message is this," cp. 1: 5. The message there spoke of the nature of God and its bearing on the Christian life. The message here instructs us as to our duty one to another. The readers heard it from the beginning, since it was among the first things inculcated in their hearts as believers, and not only so but it had been constantly repeated. Jerome informs us that toward the close of the Apostle's life, after he had become too infirm to preach, he still continued constantly to give the exhortation, "Little children, love one another." He tells us how he remarked "It is the Lord's command, and if this is done, it is enough."

What is here stated, then, is that the manifestation of the character of Christ in the believer is the outcome of receiving the Word of God. The gospel not only saves men but unites them to Christ and this produces in them that love which is essential in His character, was manifested by Him, embraces all the other qualities of the fruit of the Spirit, and fulfils the Law of God.

VERSE 12.   **not as Cain was of the Evil One, and slew his brother.**—The contrast between the children of God and the children of the Devil, having been followed by the mention of that which characterizes those who really belong to the former, leads to a typical case and the first instance of hatred to one's brother. The eighth verse recorded the beginning of the whole history of sin. Cain showed his spiritual connection with the Evil One by the slaughter of his brother. Sin, which passed into the human heart through man's wilful yielding to the suggestion of him who "sinneth from the beginning", took this form in Cain's case in spite of the Divine warning (Gen. 4: 7), and gave evidence of his moral relationship with the Evil One (see John 8: 44). The title "the Evil One" is the same as in 2: 13, where see note.

The word *sphazō*, "to slay," occurs here only in the New Testament. Originally it signified "to cut the throat"; later it came to mean "to slay violently."

And wherefore slew he him?—The form of a question is used in order to stress the evil character of the murderer, and to contrast the character of Abel. The "And" stresses the question itself (for other instances see Luke 10: 29; John 9: 36).

Because his works were evil, and his brother's righteous.—This expresses not so much the motive in Cain's heart as the nature within him; it was exhibited in his works in contrast to those of Abel, which revealed that he was righteous. The murder itself, with its immediate motive, was the outcome of that nature by which Cain "was of the Evil One." The righteousness of Abel (Heb. 11: 4) incited Cain's jealousy. The Lord sought to arrest the course of sin in Cain's heart, that he might repent of his jealousy and carry his sin no further. Probably the best translation of Genesis 4: 7 is as follows: "If thou doest well, shalt thou not be accepted? [Cain could have even then gone and brought the Divinely appointed sacrifice] and if thou doest not well [*i.e.*, refusing to do the will of God, which was still possible for him], sin coucheth at the door [*i.e.*, the sin of murder is like an animal ready to spring upon its victim], but thou shouldest rule over it." Instead of giving way to it and allowing it to gain the mastery over his heart, Cain ought to have subdued it. Instead of this he disregarded the gracious warning and allowed the sin to gain the mastery, leading him to rise up against his brother and slay him. Thus from beginning to end Cain's works were evil.

This verse concludes the mention of righteousness in this Epistle. It began at 2: 29. There has been a transition from the subject of righteousness to that of love at the close of this section (v. 10) and love now forms the central theme of the Epistle.

VERSE 13. **Marvel not, brethren, if the world hateth you.**—The Apostle now adopts a new mode of address. The title suggests the family relationship, of which love is to be the chief characteristic (see v. 11). This title occurs nowhere else in the Epistle (2: 7 should read as in the R.V.).

The preceding passage of this chapter has shown the contrasts between—

    (1) God and the Evil One,
    (2) righteousness and unrighteousness,
    (3) the children of God and the children of the Devil,

and now the last contrast is continued in the mention of the hatred of the world to God's children. Since the spirit of Cain still characterizes his moral descendants, believers are not to be surprised if the hatred that was exhibited in the murder of Abel is still manifested. The "if" does not introduce a suggestion as to what might possibly be the case, but implies the existence of the hatred as a fact. Cp. the Lord's own words in John 15: 18 and 17: 14.

Verse 14

We know—There is great stress on the pronoun, which is intended to mark emphatically a contrast between believers and the world, suggesting that, whatever the condition of the world and however hostile its attitude, that which marks believers is that they know that they have been freed from that condition.

The knowledge is intuitive, a matter of the consciousness of the fact, and not a case of progressive experience (the verb is *oida*, not *ginōskō*).

that we have passed—Perfect tense, expressing the permanent result of the past act, *i.e.* an abiding in the new state as those who have been delivered once and for all from the old.

out of death into life,—That which marks the condition of death is hatred; that which marks the condition of life is love. The change signified by the preposition *ek*, "out of", is not one of place (*apo*) but of state. To pass out of death into life is a matter of resurrection.

because we love the brethren.—This is the great test of Divine relationship. To this statement much of the teaching in the preceding part of the Epistle has led up. Briefly the steps are as follows:

True believers—

   (*a*) walk in the light (1: 7),
   (*b*) keep God's commandments (2: 3),
   (*c*) walk as Christ walked (2: 6),
   (*d*) show that they are abiding in the light by loving one another (2: 10),
   (*e*) no longer love the world and the things that are therein (2: 15),
   (*f*) practise righteousness (2: 29),
   (*g*) do not go on living in sin (3: 9),
   (*h*) exercise love (3: 14).

He that loveth not abideth in death.—Spiritual death involves the absence of spiritual love; the presence of it marks spiritual life. This closing statement of this verse makes clear that spiritual death is the condition of man by nature (Eph. 2: 1, 5). The words "his brother" in the A.V. lack valid MS. authority. It is the exercise of love in its broadest scope that is here referred to, love, that is to say, shown not merely to believers but to fellow men. "Faith worketh by love" and "faith without works is dead." He who professes faith and does not exercise love is after all in his old state of death.

VERSE 15.   **Whosoever hateth his brother is a murderer:**—The

word rendered "murderer" is, literally, "manslayer." It is found in
the N.T. only here and in John 8: 14, where it is used of the Devil.
What is stated is not to be understood merely in a moral or spiritual
sense; one who hates is thereby a would-be murderer in the physical
sense; for the motive is there though the act is not committed, and
God judges motives.

and ye know—*Oida*, as in the last verse, signifying knowledge
gained once for all and not by experience.

that no murderer hath eternal life abiding in him.—Or, more closely
to the original, "every murderer hath not . . ."; cp. 2: 19. The
destroyer of physical life is set in contrast with the possessor of
spiritual life. The statement is parallel to that at the end of verse 14;
the murderer is "he that loveth not", and, not having eternal life, he
"abideth in death." While there is forgiveness in this life for the
murderer, yet, for the destiny of him who remains in his guilt, see
Rev. 21: 8.

VERSE 16.   **Hereby know we love,**—Lit., "in this," *i.e.*, in what is
about to be stated. "Know we" is not *oida*, to know intuitively, but
the perfect tense of *ginōskō*, "we have come to know," "we have
obtained the knowledge." The A.V. "perceive" is not an adequate
rendering. The italicised words "of God," in the A.V. are not in the
original. While the love is indeed God's love, and the statement
refers to Christ, yet what is set forth is that we have come to know
love in its great, its highest expression. Love in its essence scarcely
seems to be the thought, as the concrete act of Christ's laying down
His life is immediately stated, and that act is the acme, the outstanding
exhibition, the greatest expression of love.

because He laid down His life for us:—The pronoun "He" (*ekeinos*)
bears emphasis, and points to the special character, the uniqueness,
of the One who laid down His life. Again, the order in the original is
"He for us His life laid down", and thus by setting "for us" immediately after "He", the contrast between the One who laid down His
life and those for whom He did so, is the more strikingly expressed.
    The phrase "to lay down (*tithēmi*) the life", with reference to the
Death of Christ, is confined in N.T. to the writings of John. See
John 10: 11 (R.V. "layeth down"), 15, 17, 18; 15: 13. Matthew uses
the verb "to give" (*didōmi*), Matt. 20: 28.
    Hatred found its expression in Cain's act of the murder of his

brother; love found its expression in the act of Christ on our behalf in laying down His life for us.

and we ought to lay down our lives for the brethren.—The "we" also bears stress, as if to suggest that this is the obligation especially of the followers of Christ. The verb *opheilō*, "ought", is found twice elsewhere in this Epistle, in 2: 6 and 4: 11, and again in 3 John 8, and twice in the Gospel, in 13: 14 and 19: 7. The similar word *dei*, "must", which signifies necessity rather than obligation, is not found in John's Epistles, though it occurs ten times in his Gospel.

The subject here is not that of expiatory sacrifice. That was so in the act of Christ in laying down His life, but Christ's act is here set before us as the standard for the believer in the manifestation of love. As Divine righteousness is the standard for ours (verse 7), so is Divine love for our love.

VERSE 17. **But whoso hath the world's goods,**—The "But" suggests that it would be a mistake to regard the manifestation of love as simply consisting of great and noble deeds such as laying down one's life. The greater includes the less. The test of true love lies not so much in heroic actions as in matters of daily experience and in communicating to the needs of others.

The word *bios*, "goods", is, lit., "life", and here signifies "means of living", *i.e.*, resources for the maintenance of life. *Zoē* is life as a principle; *bios* has to do more especially with the organic life of the body and its conditions.

and beholdeth his brother in need,—Literally, "having need." It is well to observe this, as the word "having" is purposely repeated after "hath the world's goods", the contrast being thus more strongly presented. The word rendered "beholdeth" (*theōreō*) signifies something more than merely seeing; it suggests a definite contemplation of the brother's circumstances. The Apostle John uses this word 23 times in the Gospel, and more frequently than any other New Testament writer, though this is the only place in his Epistles.

and shutteth up his compassion from him,—The Septuagint of Deut. 15: 7 has "Thou shalt not harden thy heart, neither shalt thou close up thy hand from thy needy brother." The word here rendered "compassion" is, literally, "bowels" (see Gen. 43: 30; 1 Kings 3: 26; Jer. 31: 20). These were regarded as the seat of the affections, and as the English equivalent is "the heart", we might render by "shutteth up his heart against him." The word is frequently used by the Apostle Paul, three times, *e.g.*, in Philemon (verses 7, 12, 20), but here only by John. The Apostle's statement suggests a determination which violates both natural feelings and Christian principles.

how doth the love of God abide in him?—By "the love of God" is primarily intended God's love to us, for He is the source of love; yet this is intended to meet with a response on our part, so that His love becomes manifested in our actions. Cp. 2: 5, and see further at 4: 20, where the aspect of our love to God is stressed, but that side is developed from what there immediately precedes rather than from the present passage. Here Divine love has been set before us in its manifestation in the act of Christ in laying down His life for us, and its effect in us is seen in our laying down our lives for one another.

VERSE 18. **My little children,**—See at verse 7. As there and elsewhere the Apostle introduces the application to practical Christian life of the teaching he has just been imparting, and the mode of address points to the solemn character of that which he is about to state.

let us not love in word, neither with the tongue;—The verb rendered "love" is in the present continuous tense, indicating what is characteristic. The next phrase is, literally, "with word and with the tongue"; this is not a mere repetition; the latter is a more intensive expression than the former. One may love in word, with a changing love to a certain extent, but it does not go far enough, it merely expresses itself in affectionate terms; but, worse still, he who loves with the tongue merely professes what he does not feel and is thus a hypocrite. That this is the difference is borne out in the phrase which follows.

but in deed and truth.—To love in deed is set in contrast to loving with word; it shows how what was to some extent genuine, but did not go far enough, is to be carried out in fulness. "And truth" is set in contrast with "with the tongue"; it speaks of what is genuine instead of what is false. But not only so, to love in truth is expressed in deeds of kindness, wrought not to one's praise, nor even with the mere idea of doing good, but genuinely in the interests of the one on whose behalf the love is shown. For this whole passage see James 2: 14–17, and Rom. 12: 9, 10.

VERSE 19. **Hereby shall we know that we are of the truth,**—The "hereby" (lit., "in this") refers to what precedes, not to what follows, as in verse 16. By exercising love in deed and truth we shall know by experience, *ginōskō*, that we are of the truth. That is to say, the truth is the source from whence springs our thoughts, motives and conduct. Cp. 2: 21, and similar language in John 3: 31; 8: 47, and the same phrase in 18: 37. There is also, however, the suggestion of a relationship established between the truth and the one who fulfils this condition, just as in the phrase "ye are of God" (4: 4) and "we are of God" (4: 6), the truth being almost, though not actually, a personification.

and shall assure our heart before Him,—The order in the original is "and before Him we shall assure our heart." "Before Him" is put first for emphasis, and thus stresses the fact that it is in His presence that the experience is enjoyed, a circumstance impossible for the one who refuses to exercise love and compassion. Practical love is the working of the Divine life, producing the assurance in one's heart that he is of the truth. The singular "our heart" is undoubtedly right here; it lays stress upon the individual aspect of the experience rather than that of believers generally. The heart here stands, not for the seat of affection, but for the conscience, as also in Acts 2: 37; 7: 45.*

The word rendered "assure" is, literally, "persuade", which is almost invariably its meaning, but in this passage, the only occurrence of the word in John's writings, the sense seems to be rather that of convincing.

VERSE 20. **whereinsoever our heart condemn us; because God is greater than our heart, and knoweth all things.**—It will be noted that the R.V. continues in this verse the sentence in verse 19, making the phrase "whereinsoever our heart condemn us" depend upon the word "persuade". That is to say, if we have something upon our conscience by which we are self-condemned, such as failure to exercise love, "God is greater than our heart and knows all things", and the Apostle has already shown how, through the efficacy of the blood of Christ, we may be cleansed from our sin and enjoy fellowship with God (1: 7, 9; 2: 1). The rendering in the A.V., "and shall assure our hearts before Him. For if our heart condemn us, God is greater than our heart, and knoweth all things", gives very much the same thought as the R.V. but does not take account of the fact that in the original there is a conjunction (*hoti*, "that" or "because"). That is to say,

* For a list see *Expository Dictionary of New Testament Words*, section Vol. II, p. 206 (by W. E. Vine).

taking the text on which the R.V. is based, there is a conjunction (*hoti*) at the beginning of verse 20, and this is repeated after "condemn us". Many suggestions have been made in order to overcome the difficulty, but none of them are as satisfactory as the R.V. It seems best then to adhere to that Version. The great facts are plain. By showing practical love we know that we are of the truth, and, further, in the presence of God we are confirmed and assured. Having nothing on our conscience we have confidence before Him. Even if we, like Peter, may think that others may perceive but little love, it is a mercy to realize the Lord's omniscience. Whether we are conscious of failure or not, God is greater than our heart and knows all things. This should lead us to remember that, even if we have a conscience void of offence, there may be something which God knows, and, on the other hand, if there is something upon our conscience, it can be put right before Him who knows all about us. The great thing is to be happy in God's presence.

The word signifying "condemn" is *kataginōskō*, (lit., "to know against," a compound form of *ginōskō*, to know). This similarity of form may perhaps be brought out in this way, that "whatever we know against ourselves God knows all things."

That God is greater than our heart probably means that He is greater in the matter of judgment, and that He knows the character of our sin absolutely. It may mean also that He is greater in the matter of compassion, and so we have the assurance that we are in the hands of One who deals with man in compassion as well as in His absolute knowledge.

VERSE 21. **Beloved,**—See 2:7, R.V.; 3:2; 4:1; 4:7.

if our heart condemn us not, we have boldness toward God;—That is, we are able to look up to God in freedom from dismay and terror, enjoying the consciousness of His approval, and that fellowship with Him which brings His peace and power into our lives. For "boldness" see note on 2:28. With the expression "toward God" cp. Acts 24:16. Boldness towards God is the effect of the assurance of heart mentioned in verse 19. On the other hand, the effect of the boldness itself is given in verse 22.

VERSE 22. **and whatsoever we ask, we receive of Him,**—The "and" probably connects this verse with the preceding by way of explanation, pointing out the character as well as the effect of our boldness. We have freedom in asking and likewise the assurance of the effectiveness of our prayers. The primary condition for this, then, is freedom from the consciousness of sin (verse 21). There must be no distance between God and us. The present tense of the verbs in this and the preceding verses indicates a continuance of the conditions referred to. To have boldness towards God and to receive from Him what we ask should be normal with us. See Matt. 7: 7, 8: John 14: 13; 15: 16; 16: 23, 24. The word signifying ask (*aiteō*) is found in this Epistle only; see 5: 14, 15, 16. In the last mentioned verse a different word is rendered "make request."

We may not see immediately the answer to our prayer. The granting is immediate, but the fulfilment may be a matter of waiting some considerable time. Faith leads us to await God's time.

because we keep His commandments, and do the things that are pleasing in His sight.—This presents a condition upon which our prayer is answered, and follows in line with verse 22. Obedience to God and conformity with His will are pre-requisites to the reception of the answers to our prayers, though this does not involve any merit on our part as a ground upon which God shows us favour (see John 9: 31; Job 27: 8, 9; Psa. 66: 18, 19; Prov. 15: 29; Isa. 1: 15). The reason is not far to seek, for the one who is in the enjoyment of communion with God and fulfils His will, will make only those requests which are in accordance with His will.

Doing the things that are pleasing in His sight is more than keeping His commandments. The latter is included in the former. The practice of God's will is a higher standard than obedience to precepts, and the believer is to seek to do that in which God delights as well as to obey what He commands. Obedience may be a matter merely of subjection; doing the things that are pleasing to Him is a matter of love. See John 8: 29.

The phrase "in His sight" is to be distinguished from "before Him" at the end of verse 19. "Before Him" gives prominence to our attitude toward God; "in His sight" conveys more prominently the thought of the regard that God graciously pays to us.

VERSE 23. **And this is His commandment, that we should believe in the name of His Son Jesus Christ, and love one another,**—The conjunction *hina*, "that", introduces, not the purpose of the commandment, but an explanation of its nature and requirement. That faith is put as the basis of conduct strikes a blow at the contention of those who would advocate that as long as one does what is right it does not matter what he believes. On the contrary, again and again faith is laid down as the basis of action. Right living depends upon right thinking and, for the Christian, right thinking is necessarily a matter of faith. Again, what is here set forth is that true faith is expressed in right conduct. "Faith worketh by love." "Faith if it have not works is dead in itself" (Jas. 2: 17, and see the whole section, verses 14–26).

The tense of the verbs rendered "believing" and "love" is the continuous present and expresses habits of thought and deed.

The phrase rendered "believe in the name" has no preposition in the original, and is literally "believe the name", which signifies to believe all that is implied in His Name, that is to say, Christ's Divine relationship, attributes and functions, His character and operations; these are conveyed by the threefold title "His Son", "Jesus", "Christ."

even as He gave us commandment.—All His commandments are summed up in the one injunction concerning love (see John 13: 34; 15: 12, 17). Faith in Christ and love to one another are spoken of as one commandment. The two are obviously to be regarded as inseparable, and this is exhibited in the teaching of the Lord as recorded constantly in the Gospel of John. The exercise of love forms an essential part of the activity of faith in Christ; it is the outward expression of the inward reality of faith.

This 23rd verse thus provides an expansion of the subject of the "new commandment" in 2: 8.

VERSE 24. **And he that keepeth His commandments**—The participial phrase "he that keepeth" describes what is to be the characteristic habit of the believer.

The plural, "His commandments", takes us back to verse 22, which speaks of keeping His commandments. Verse 23 is somewhat parenthetic, yet there is an intimation in verse 24 that Christ, who "gave us commandment", is also now spoken of in the pronouns His, Him and He, there being no sharp distinction drawn between the Divine Persons.

abideth in Him, and He in him.—Connect with this 2: 28 and 2: 3, and see notes at each place for the significance. This abiding in, or indwelling, suggests the most intimate union, and the indwelling is mutual, as in John 15: 4. That it is an abiding both in the Father and in the Son, is clear from John 17: 21, 23, 26. This holy association is not the result of keeping God's commandments; on the contrary the latter is the result of the mutual indwelling, and a testimony to its existence.

And hereby—Lit., "in this", as in 2: 3, 5; 3: 16, 19; 4: 9, 10, 13, 17 and 5: 2. Probably the reference here is to what follows.

we know that He abideth in us,—We know by experience (*ginōskō*). The Apostle does not repeat "and we in Him", but it is implied from what has preceded.

by the Spirit which He gave us.—This is the first actual mention of the Holy Spirit in the Epistle, though the anointing mentioned in 2: 20 and 27 was figurative of His Person and work. Believers were there said to have received Him and to possess Him; here He is mentioned as the One who was given to them. The word rendered "gave" is in the aorist tense, pointing to the definite occasion upon which the Holy Spirit was given. He is received by the believer at the moment when he believes on the Lord Jesus Christ. The Spirit is there and the seal of God's work in the heart of the believer, and the earnest, or pledge, of his future inheritance: "in whom (that is, Christ), having also believed, ye were sealed with the Holy Spirit of promise, which is an earnest of our inheritance" (Eph. 1: 13, 14—the A.V., "after that ye believed" is misleading; there is no preposition in the original, the sealing is simultaneous with believing). It should be noted in Acts 19: 2 that the disciples whom Paul found in Ephesus had not heard whether the Holy Ghost "was given" (not as in A.V. "whether there be any Holy Ghost"; they knew of His existence but did not know what had taken place at Pentecost).

This is the fourth evidence of the new life in the believer. They are as follows:—

(1) keeping God's commandments (2: 4),
(2) the doing of righteousness (2: 29),
(3) loving in deeds as well as word (3:18),
(4) the possession of the Spirit (3: 24).

The following are mentioned in this Epistle as abiding in the believer:

(1) the word of God (2: 14),
(2) the anointing (2: 27),
(3) the seed (3: 9),
(4) the love of God (3: 17),
(5) God Himself (3: 24; 4: 12, 13, 15),
(6) Christ (implied in 3: 24). See also John 6: 56 and 15: 5.

CHAPTER IV

ANALYSIS OF CHAPTER IV

(A) Verses 1–6—The Spirit of Truth and the Spirit of Error.

(B) Verses 7–21—God's Love in Christ and His Children's Response.

(A) Verses 1–6

Verses

(1) A warning 1

 (a) Negative—against believing every spirit
 (b) Positive—to prove the spirits
 (c) The reason—the many false prophets.

(2) The first means of distinguishing: viz., by a person's attitude toward the truth concerning Christ 2, 3a

 (a) The Personal Source:

  1. The Spirit of God 2a
  2. The spirit of the Antichrist 3b

 (b) The resulting confession, derived from the Personal Source:

  1. The Spirit which is of God confesses that Jesus Christ is come in the flesh 2b

  2. The spirit which is not of God confesses not Jesus: 3a

   (i) Its future advent
   (ii) Its present existence

(3) The distinction confirmed: 4, 5

 (a) The readers themselves: 4

  1. Their Divine nature—they are of God 4a

  2. Their victory—they have overcome the world 4a

  3. The reason—the Spirit in them is greater than the spirit in the world 4b

Chapter IV. (A) Verses 1-6

Introductory Note

The Apostle now seeks to give his readers a means of assurance that what has been ministered is the truth, in contrast to the errors advanced by false teachers. He shews that there are two spirits in the world, and sets these in sharp contrast. The one is the Holy Spirit who abides in the believer, as mentioned at the end of the 3rd chapter. The other is the spirit of the Antichrist which is in the world. The one is the Spirit of truth, the other is the spirit of error. We are to be assured as to whether we are being led by the Spirit of God, or by the spirit of error. We are therefore to prove the spirits whether they are of God, that is, whether they proceed from God. The main connection between this chapter and the preceding one is that, Chapter 3 shows the necessity of proving our relationship to God by our actions; the beginning of Chapter 4 continues the theme, but puts it another way, namely, that confession of truth attests the fact of relationship to God. The immediate connection between the two chapters lies in the mention of the Spirit of God.

VERSE 1. **Beloved,**—See note at 3: 21.

believe not every spirit,—This is set in contrast to the mention of the Holy Spirit at the end of the preceding chapter. While we have the assurance that Christ abides in us by the Spirit which He gave us, yet we are to be on our guard against deceptive spirits. Our assurance should be the means of increasing our powers of discernment in regard to contrary influences. The tense of the verb is continuous, it suggests that we are to be in the habit of refusing to believe every spirit. Not that all who come to teach us are to be regarded as false simply because we are unacquainted with them and their antecedent associations. There must be discernment.

but prove the spirits,—*Dokimazō*, "to try", is to be distinguished from *peirazō*, a word with a similar meaning. That they resemble one another is evident from their association in 2 Cor. 13: 5, and Psa. 25: 2 in the LXX. John rarely uses either. This is the only place where *dokimazō* is found in his writings. *Peirazō* which is frequent in the New Testament he uses only four times (John 6: 6; Rev. 2: 2, 10; 3: 10). *Dokimazō* is never used in the sense of proving, as is the case of *peirazō*. Broadly speaking the proving signified by *dokimazō* suggests a good motive, the hope that what is tested will stand the test, whereas *peirazō* frequently suggests the hope that what is tested will be found wanting. Though this is not always the case, for *peirazō* is used once of God in Heb. 11:17, and once of the Lord Jesus (John 6: 6), with whom the purpose always is the benefit of the one who is tested. As an example of the former see 1 Thess. 5: 21. So here the object of the command to prove the spirits is to see whether they are of God, so that what is of God may be accepted and what is not of God may be rejected. While the proving of spirits is itself a spiritual gift (1 Cor. 12: 10), yet all believers are responsible to form a judgment concerning spiritual things, and, as the Apostle has pointed out, provision has been made for this under the "anointing from the Holy One" (2: 18, 20, 27; cp. 2 Tim. 2: 7). Yet the power of spiritual perception depends on the spiritual state and conduct of the believer in response to the anointing. Discernment of the truth belongs only to the godly (Prov. 28: 5; Dan. 9: 13; 2 Pet. 1: 9).

Moreover, the desire to be impressed, to have the feelings wrought upon, rather than to be instructed in the ways of the Lord, is a common snare to the saints (2 Tim. 3:6, 7; 4: 3, 4).

The completed Scriptures, *i.e.*, the O.T. and N.T., became later the sole and sufficient standard by which all teaching oral or written could be tested, but long before that time believers and churches had multiplied widely. During the intervening period, in the case of revelations, for the testing of which the O.T. was not available, such as that referred to in Col. 1: 26, *e.g.,*, believers were encouraged, by the promised guidance of the Holy Spirit, John 16: 13, to compare utterances claiming to be spiritual, 1 Cor. 2: 13, and so to test the prophecy and the spirit that prompted it, 1 Cor. 14: 29; 1 John 4: 6; Rev. 2: 2."

whether they are of God;—That is, whether they have God as their source. The claim of any authority to Divine doctrine must be tested by the Scriptures, which, as they themselves testify, have their origin in God. Gal. 1: 8, 9 makes clear that no new revelation was to be added. Neither the dictates of the Church nor those of conscience are a sufficient guide as to Divine truth and the will of God. Conscience may be entirely mistaken. Church dictates may consist of accretions to the faith. We must neither mistake self-will for conscience nor accept doctrines which add to, or detract from, the Word of God.

because many false teachers are gone out into the world.—Cp. 2: 18. The false prophets here spoken of include the antichrists there mentioned as having already arisen. Christ had foretold that false prophets would arise, and similar warning had been given in the Epistles (Matt. 7: 15; 24: 4, 5, 24; 1 Tim. 4: 1; 2 Tim. 3: 13; 4: 3, *e.g.*) The false teachers, of which the Apostle had already spoken in 2: 18, had identified themselves with believers before they went out from their midst. Those referred to here were apparently more numerous and had arisen in other ways. They include those who had not professed the Christian faith, as well as the more dangerous type who had done so. That they are said to have gone out into the world suggests their having had a mission from spiritual powers of darkness, whose object is to deceive men. The "world" stands for the mass of unregenerate humanity, which lies in the evil one. The purpose of wicked spirits, through their human agents, would be to maintain unbelievers in a state of alienation from God, and to lead astray the saints. The perfect tense "have gone out" suggests that the evil influence had come to stay.

VERSE 2.   **Hereby know ye the Spirit of God:**—"Hereby" is literally "in this", as frequently elsewhere in the Epistle (*e.g.*, 3: 16, 19, 24). The phrase points to what follows, which provides believers with the necessary test. The verb for "know" is *ginōskō*, and the meaning is "you know by experience of facts and so are able to recognize." The experience is comprehensive and belongs to all true believers. The Spirit of God is to be recognized as a result of trying the spirits, and the nature of any testimony will be recognized by its agreement with the doctrines of the faith once for all delivered to the saints, of which the Holy Saint is the source.

every spirit which confesseth that Jesus Christ is come in the flesh is of God:—The phrase "every spirit" does not refer to other beings than human, but to the person whose spirit is acted upon by the Holy Spirit, through whose instrumentality he confesses the truth. It is to be noted that the Apostle says "in the flesh", not "into the flesh." The statement is directed against the Gnostic error promulgated by Cerinthus, that the Christ descended into an already existing man. As the Gospel states, "the Word became flesh" (1: 14, R.V., not "was made", as in the A.V.). Christ "was born of the seed of David according to the flesh" (Rom. 1: 3, R.V., not "was made", as in the A.V.). Cp. Gal. 4: 4, R.V. Christ partook of flesh and blood (Heb. 2: 14).

It is possible to render the original as follows: "every Spirit that confesseth that Jesus is Christ having come in flesh", or again "con-

fesseth Jesus Christ having come in flesh." All the Gnostic sects
denied this truth. They maintained a distinction between Christ
(whom they called an æon) and the man Jesus. The Apostle maintains
the truth that Jesus Christ is one inseparable Person and that He has
become flesh. Cp. Col. 2: 9.

The perfect tense "having come" should be noted. It represents an
abiding effect. From His Incarnation onward Christ was, and ever is,
possessed of true Manhood. Involved in this is the truth that He is the
"one Mediator between God and Man, Himself Man, Christ Jesus"
(1 Tim. 2: 5, R.V.). Every spirit who confesses this truth is of God,
i.e., is derived from God, the person himself having been born of
God. See 2: 16; 3: 10, and John 8: 47.

VERSE 3.   **and every spirit which confesseth not Jesus is not of
God:**—The R.V. is to be taken as correct, according to the most
authentic MSS. The confession of "Jesus" includes what has been
said in verse 2, while specially stressing the Lord's humanity. For
other occasions of the use of the single title see Rom. 3: 26; 10: 9;
1 Thess. 4: 14; Heb. 2: 9, etc.

and this is the spirit of the antichrist,—Though the word "spirit" is
not in the original, something must be supplied, and this is undoubtedly the best insertion after what has been said in verse 2. The
Antichrist will deny the truth relating to Christ, as he will not merely
be opposed to Christ but will be Satan's substitute for Him. See 2: 22,
23 and notes there.

whereof ye have heard that it cometh;—That is, the spirit of the
Antichrist, the spirit that opposes Christ, substituting another
instead of Him. The personal Antichrist will indeed come, but what
the Apostle next says shews that he has in view the antichristian spirit.
The present tense "cometh" expresses the fact that such a spirit
would be present, and would issue in the advent of the Antichrist
himself. This the Apostle had taught the saints when he was with
them.

and now it is in the world already.—"Already" is put last to add
stress. Cp. John 4: 35, where the original puts "already" last in the
sentence. Here the word gives an intimation that, while the spirit of
the Antichrist is present in the world, something more is to follow.
The spirit which is now present is preparing the way for the Antichrist himself. Cp. what the Apostle Paul says about "the mystery of

lawlessness" in 2 Thess. 2: 7, where the stress is on the word "law-lessness."

VERSE 4. **Ye are of God, my little children,**—The "ye" is emphatic and is thus set in marked contrast to the false prophets (verse 1). Inasmuch as the Apostle has said that every spirit that confesseth that Jesus Christ is come in the flesh "is of God" (verse 2), and now he says, "ye are of God", his readers are one in Divine relationship with those who have taught them the truth. For the mode of address see note at 2: 1, 12, etc.

and have overcome them:—That is to say, the false teachers. The overcoming consists in having refused to listen to them. The fact that the antichristian spirit is in the world, means conflict for the children of God and victory for the faithful. It also means their practical identification with Christ, Who said, "Be of good cheer; I have overcome the world" (John 16: 33). See also John 10: 5.

because greater is He that is in you than he that is in the world.—The power for victory lies, not in the child of God himself, but in the One who indwells Him. The realization of this gives triumphant confidence in face of spiritual foes, confidence, not in self, but in God. See Zech. 4: 6; 1 Cor. 15: 57; Eph. 6: 10.

"He that is in you" is the Holy Spirit; "he that is in the world" is the evil one, "the prince of this world" (John 12: 31), "the god of this world" (2 Cor. 4: 4). Cp. John 8:44. In the strength, then, of "the Spirit which God gave us" (3: 24) we are to fight against the influence which permeates that system of human society which lies in spiritual darkness and is organized, socially, intellectually and morally, by the evil one and his hosts, against God and His Christ.

VERSE 5. **They are of the world:**—"They" are the false teachers; cp. 2: 18. Their character and teaching are derived from that spirit which is in the world. The word "they" has special stress, just as "ye" had at the beginning of verse 4.

therefore speak they as of the world, and the world heareth them.—The character of their teachings is consistent with their evil origin, and what they teach meets with a ready reception on the part of those who belong to the same system. The world loves its own (John 15: 19) Compare and contrast 17: 14. Again, "he that is of the earth is of the earth, and of the earth he speaketh" (John 3: 31, R.V.). There is stress upon the phrase "of the world"; the order in the original is "therefore of the world they speak." The meaning is not that they speak concerning, or about, the world, but that the world is the element which characterizes their utterances. The same spirit energizes both teachers and hearers.

VERSE 6. **We are of God:**—This is set in contrast with the statement in verse 5. In verse 4 the Apostle predicated the same thing of his readers (see note there). As, then, the one antichristian spirit energizes the false prophets and their words (verse 5), so, on the contrary. the Holy Spirit energizes both the teachers of the truth and the children of God who are taught by them. The Apostle has something more to say, however, about the latter and this he now states. The "we" is again emphatic.

he that knoweth God heareth us; he who is not of God heareth us not.—The Apostle does not say "he that is of God" but "he that knoweth God" directing the reader to the effect of being born again. The verb "knoweth" is *"ginōskō"* indicating the knowledge gained by progressive experience. Again the construction of the article with the present participle, lit., "the one knowing", is a description expressive of a habit; that is to say, the one who habitually is getting to know God; cp. 5: 20. The change from "he that is of God" to "he that knoweth God" suggests at once that the child of God is one who enters upon the progressive experience of knowing Him.

The Apostle's statement plainly reveals his consciousness of the Divine authority imparted to him and to his fellow-apostles. It also implies the Divine inspiration of their writings.

By this—Lit., "from this", not "in this", as elsewhere in this Epistle, *e.g.*, 2: 5; 3: 16, etc. This is the only place where this particular phrase occurs in the Epistle. It refers to what has just preceded, and introduces an inference therefrom.

we know—*Ginōskō* again, as in the preceding part of the verse; that is to say, we are constantly experiencing the knowledge.

the spirit of truth, and the spirit of error.—The Spirit of truth is the Holy Spirit, as in John 14: 17; 15: 26; 16: 13. Paul speaks of Him as "the Spirit which is of God" (1 Cor. 2: 12). The phrase "the Spirit of truth" may describe either:

(1) the source from whence He has proceeded, as sent from the Father (John 14: 26) and from the Son (16: 7), or

(2) His character as the One Who is truth, or

(3) The One Who communicates the truth (John 16: 13, 14); (2) and (3) are closely associated and together seem to convey what is intended. The spirit of error or of deceit, a phrase found here only in the New Testament, is the spirit which is characterized by, and communicates, error, which comes from him of whom the Lord said that "he is a liar and the father thereof" (John 8: 44). Cp. 2: 22; 2 Thess. 2: 10 and 1 Tim. 4: 1. Those who are children of God learn to know the Spirit of truth and the spirit of error, according to the way in which any teaching conforms, or otherwise, to the teaching of the Apostles.

(B) Verses 7–21

Introductory Note

The resumption of the subject of brotherly love is not by way of a sharp break from what has immediately preceded. On the contrary it is closely connected with it, inasmuch as the Spirit of truth produces love, whereas the spirit of error is ever against it. Love proceeds from God. The antichristian spirit is selfish. In the first of the three parts of the Epistle which deal with brotherly love, this was shown to be the characteristic, as well as the effect, of walking in the light (2: 7–11). Secondly, it was set forth as a characteristic of God's children and a mark of their righteous conduct (3: 10–18). Here it is shown to proceed from God as being essentially His attribute, and as having been manifested by Him in Christ. Connected with this is the fact that God sent His Son to be the Saviour of the world.

VERSE 7. **Beloved, let us love one another:**—For the form of address see note at 2: 7 etc. The mutual love of believers is here in view, as the context makes clear.

for love is of God;—Verse 4 stated "Ye are of God"; verse 6 "We are of God." Therefore from the statement that "love is of God" the inference is clear that love is a uniting bond of the heavenly family.

and everyone that loveth is begotten of God, and knoweth God.— Since love has God as its source, those who show the love that is here spoken of give evidence thereby that they are the children of God. Their spiritual life is derived from Him. The verb rendered "is begotten" is in the perfect tense, and is better translated "has been begotten", suggesting the abiding effects of the new relationship. "Everyone that loveth; . . . knoweth God." To exhibit Divine love is an evidence of more than the existence of the Divine relationship; it is a proof of the experience of a constant increase in the knowledge of God (*ginōskō*, see notes on verse 6). This connection between knowing God and exercising love recalls the similar connection in 2: 3-5.

VERSE 8. **He that loveth not knoweth not God;**—In the contrast here presented there is a change in the tense of the verb "to know." In verse 7 it was in the present continuous tense; here the aorist or point tense is used, literally, "did not know God", referring to the time when the supposed new relationship began. The new birth, however, was never experienced in such a case, nor did he who does not manifest love ever know God. See the closing statement of 3: 1, and cp. John 16: 3. The Apostle does not repeat the subject of being begotten of God, he does not say "he that loveth not has not been begotten of God", he passes at once to the comprehensive statement "noweth not God", which involves the absence of the new birth.

for God is love.—This is a deeper truth than what was expressed at the beginning of verse 7. That predicated what the source of love was; this predicates the nature of God Himself. It does not convey, however, that God is simply loving and benevolent, nor that His love is merely a quality which He possesses; it is His essential nature, and it is for this special reason that one who does not exercise love has not been born of God and does not know Him.

This is the second statement in this Epistle, of the nature of God. In 1: 5 the Apostle declared that "God is light." Just as light is His very nature, so is love. That God is love is a truth unknown to heathen nations, and it was but imperfectly realized in the Jewish religion as such.

VERSE 9. **Herein was the love of God manifested in us,**—"Herein" is literally "in this." See notes on 3: 16 and 3: 19. Obviously the phrase here refers to what follows, introducing a statement as to how the nature of God, in the respect mentioned, was particularly exhibited. It was not merely manifested towards us, we ourselves are the sphere in which it is exhibited. This meaning of the phrase is confirmed by verse 12 below, which states that mutual love is a proof of the indwelling of God and of the perfecting of His love "in us."

that God hath sent His only begotten Son into the world, that we might live through Him.—The perfect tense, "hath sent", signifies the abiding results of Christ's mission (contrast the aorists, or point, tenses "loved" and "sent", in verse 10 below).

The word *monogenēs*, "only-begotten," is found only in the writings of the Apostle John, four times in the Gospel (1: 14, 18; 3: 16, 18) and here. In the Septuagint, however, the word is used to translate a Hebrew word which it also renders in other places by *agapētos*, "beloved." Thus Gen. 22: 2 reads "thy son, the beloved one"; so again in verses 12 and 16. Psalm 22: 20 has *monogenēs*, "only-begotten one"; so in Psa. 35: 17 (margin, "My only One"). The title "only-begotten" speaks of the eternal relationship of the Son to the Father, and at the same time expresses the Father's delight in the Son. It is a term used absolutely of Christ in His Divine relationship, whereas the title "Firstborn", while used of Christ in distinction from all creatures absolutely, yet bears reference to them. The thought of love and delight must not be lost sight of in considering the word "only-begotten", though the eternal relationship needs also to be borne in mind.

He it was, as so described, whom God sent into the world. The stress in the original, placed upon the word "only-begotten", should be noted—"His Son, His Only-Begotten." The definite article is used before "Son" and "Only-Begotten", and gives prominence to both relationships. This is so also in the Gospel, 3: 16.

that we might live through Him.—This, in addition to the fact just mentioned regarding the Person sent, is what makes the love of God unique. But for this act of infinite mercy we should have remained in spiritual darkness and have been consigned to the Second Death. To such a doom the word "live" is set in contrast, but it carries with it also all that is comprehended in the life imparted, namely, the qualities and activities which are involved therein and are manifested, for instance, by the exercise of love one to another (see verse 11). The life imparted through Him is maintained by Him. The conspicuous thought, however, is the impartation of life, and this is indicated by the use of the aorist, or point, tense of the verb.

VERSE 10. **Herein is love, not that we loved God, but that He loved us,**—"Herein" is literally "in this," pointing to what follows and specifying the particular fact in which love, in its essence and perfection, was exhibited. The absolute spontaneity of the love of God is seen not only in the fact that God is love (verse 8), that is so indeed, but in this also, that there was no quality in man to elicit that love; on the contrary there was an absence in the human heart of that which was due to God. Whatever love there is in us by reason of the new life imparted, is the outcome of, and a response to, His love.

and sent His Son to be the propitiation for our sins.—Here there is a change from the perfect tense, "hath seen" in verse 9, to the aorist tense, thus stressing the historical fact of the sending. For the subject of Christ as the propitiation for our sins see 2: 2 and notes thereon. Here the Apostle takes us back to what is antecedent to the gift of life. As he showed in chapter 1, the sin question must be settled before life is bestowed. In sending his Only-Begotten Son that we might live through Him, the design was that He might first be the propitiation for our sins. What the Apostle here says, then, is the great evidence that (1) "love is of God" (verse 7) and (2) "God is love" (verse 8).

VERSE 11. **Beloved,**—This is the sixth and last time in the Epistle in which the readers are so addressed. There is no further mode of address till the last verse of the Epistle. See 2: 7 (R.V.); 3: 2; 4: 1; 4: 7.

if God so loved us,—The stress of the sentence is on the word "so", as is seen in the order in the original, "if so God loved us." The "if" is not merely supposition, it is virtually equivalent to "since." Cp. for instance the "if" in John 13: 14, and the parallel clause that follows there.

we also ought to love one another.—This presents the practical conclusion from the double statement of the reason why God sent His Son, and resumes the exhortation in verse 7. What was there given as an exhortation, is here presented as an obligation, a debt. The order "we also", in the R.V., should be noted. The "also" is to be attached to the "we." That is to say, "we, as well as God." In other words, we should be "like God," to manifest His nature and follow His example. This obligation rests, then, on the great foundation truth of the Atonement.

VERSE 12. **No man hath beheld God at any time:**—This is not quite the same statement as in John 1: 18. The R.V. correctly marks the distinction by the rendering "beheld." In John 1: 18 the word is simply "to see", and the declaration there is that God is invisible.

Cp. 1 Tim. 6: 16. Here, however, the verb implies contemplation, something of more comprehensive character than merely seeing. In both statements the stress is on the word "God", which in each case stands first in the sentence in the original.

The Apostle seems to break off abruptly here from the subject in verse 11, but this is only apparent; for the statements in the end of verse 12, which continue the subject of verse 11, are introduced by what the Apostle says in this sentence. For the connection see the following notes.

if we love one another, God abideth in us, and His love is perfected in us:—The connection with the preceding statement seems to be somewhat as follows: "While for anyone to behold God is an impossibility, and His presence is not discernible by contemplation, yet we may have the definite experience of His very presence, and this experience is made good in our case if we love one another. Moreover, His presence is not simply external, for He abides in us. He is not simply existent but resident. More still, since God is love, it follows that if we love one another, as is enjoined in His Word, His love has been perfected in us" (the original has the perfect tense).

"His love" is not simply our love to Him, nor again is it simply His love to man; the meaning seems to be that the love which characterizes Him (verse 8), and has been manifested by Him (verse 9), finds its expression and counterpart in the love which we exercise, and thus His love is perfected; that is to say, it reaches its fulfilment, in us. That this is the meaning is confirmed by verses 16 and 17 below.

Accordingly, though we cannot behold God, yet the great expression of His very nature is manifested in and by us, and demonstrates, not only His existence, but the fact that He dwells in us and that His character of love is developed and fulfilled in our case.

VERSE 13.   **hereby know we that we abide in Him, and He in us,** because He hath given us of His Spirit.—Literally, "in this we know", *ginōskō*, that is, we know by continuous experience. This statement is parallel to, and a slight expansion of, the latter part of 3: 24, where see notes. There is an addition in regard to the statement of our experience, in that the Apostle now says that we know "that we abide in Him." Though he had put it as a matter of fact in the first part of 3: 24, the twofold fact is put here as a matter of experience, both that we abide in Him and He in us.

There is another change, too, from 3: 24. The Spirit was there stated as the Source of our experience. Here the fact that God has given us of His Spirit, is proof in our experience that we abide in Him and He in us. Further, in 3: 24 the gift of the Spirit was connected with the keeping of His commandments; here it is connected with the exercise of love. There is, however, practically no distinction in this respect, as he who manifests love has fulfilled the Law.

The statement that God has given us of His Spirit does not mean that He gives the Spirit by measure or in portions; it is definitely stated in John 3: 34 that He does not do this (the words "unto him" in the A.V. of that verse are not part of the original). The significance of the phrase "of His Spirit", seems to be, that, while each child of God has the Holy Spirit, the love which we manifest is the outcome of that gift. In other words, the exercise of love is involved in the possession of the Spirit.

VERSE 14. **And we have beheld and bear witness that the Father hath sent the Son to be the Saviour of the world.**—Verses 14 and 15 explain the whole of the first 12 verses of the chapter. The word rendered "beheld" is the same as in verse 12, and the connection is somewhat as follows: "While no man hath beheld God at any time, yet the Apostles had seen the Son of God, Whom the Father had sent to be the Saviour of the world, and Who, being the Son of the Father, combined manhood with Deity, and is the great expression of God's love. As, then, God has manifested His love in Christ, we are to show the same nature, the spirit of love, and this is possible only because the Holy Spirit, Who proceeds from the Father, dwells in us. By this means God still reveals Himself through us. The Apostles, in companying with the Son of God in the days of His flesh, and subsequently to His resurrection, had themselves received personal evidence of this. To it they were bearing witness. Accordingly, through their testimony we are to continue to bear the same witness." The "we" at the beginning of the verse bears stress and signifies John and his fellow-Apostles.

This verse states that the Father sent the Son; verses 9 and 10 state that God sent Him. In verses 9 and 10 the Godhood of the Son is prominent. He is "His only-begotten Son" (verse 9). Here in verse 14 the stress is upon His Sonship; He is "the Son." The perfect tense "hath sent" intimates not merely the historic fact but the abiding effects of the sending.

Only twice in John's writings does he use the title "Saviour", here in verse 14 and in the Gospel, 4:42, and in each place He is spoken of as "the Saviour of the world."

That Christ is described as "the Saviour of the world" was a testimony against the national prejudice and exclusivism of the Jews, as well as against the circumscribed and erroneous ideas of any particular sect such as the Gnostics. The scope of His mission was as boundless as humanity, and only man's impenitence and unbelief put a limit to its actual effect.

VERSE 15. **Whosoever shall confess that Jesus is the Son of God, God abideth in Him, and he in God.**—There is a connection with verse 2. The confession referred to there was in respect of the real humanity of Christ; here it has to do with His Divine Sonship. In verse 2 the point was the unity of essence and counsel between the Father and the Son (cp. 2: 23); here confession of Jesus as Son of God is a token of a life that is united to Him. There the confession served to differentiate those who are of God and those who are of the world, and who are influenced by the spirit of the Antichrist; here confession serves to differentiate between those who give evidence by their love that they are children of God and those who, however much they profess, do not manifest love, and are liars. In each place the confession is shown to be produced by the Holy Spirit, and here it involves the same spirit of love as was manifested by Christ, and a life that bears testimony to His saving power.

There could be no closer communion or relationship than what is expressed in the statement "God abideth in him and he in God"; cp. 3: 24; the similar statement there, which is said of the one who keeps God's commandments, and that in 4: 16, show how inseparably associated are doctrine and practice. Cp. also John 6: 56; 14:20; 15; 4, 5.

The aorist tense of the verb rendered "confesseth" conveys the thought, not so much of time, as of decisiveness in the confession.

VERSE 16. **And we know and have believed the love which God hath in us.**—The "we", which bears stress, refers to all believers, as being those mentioned in the preceding verse, who are characterized by the confession that Jesus is the Son of God. Alternatively it refers to the Apostles, but the context suggests the former application. More closely to the original we may render by "We have come to know and have believed", that is to say, "we have entered upon a path of progressive knowledge" (*ginōskō*). In one aspect of the case faith precedes knowledge, and knowledge perfects faith; for faith is necessary to apprehend the things of God. On the other hand, the knowledge which implies personal acquaintance with Christ and experience of His will and way, is necessary for the perfecting of faith. That is perhaps why knowledge is put first here. While, then, there is an elementary faith which precedes knowledge, there is a practical faith which puts knowledge into effect. For the opposite order see the remarks of the disciples, as recorded in John 6: 69, "We have believed and know." There it had to do with a fact of Divine truth; this has to do with the experience of Divine love,—not merely the knowledge of the fact that God loves us, but the experience of God's love in us, by which we so know God's nature that we love one another. This is the work of the Holy Spirit in us (cp. verse 13).

God is love; and he that abideth in love abideth in God, and God abideth in him.—That God is love expresses His nature as made known to us in Christ. In verse 8 the statement "God is love" was used as an argument to press home the duty of walking in love, and the development of that argument leads to a reiteration of the statement here with an expanded context. The development of the argument is as follows: The duty of walking in love because God is love, was confirmed by the proof of it. The first detail in the proof was the fact of the sending of God's Son (verse 9); the second was in the propitiation He made for sin (verse 10); the third was in the inward witness of the Spirit, giving us the experience of His power, which includes (1) the witness of the Apostles that the Father sent the Son to be the Saviour of the world, (2) the impartation of the Divine nature and union with God to all those who confess that Jesus is His Son, (3) the practical knowledge of the love of God as working in the believer. All that line of proof leads up, then, to a renewal of the statement that "God is love", and now the Apostle immediately shows that only by abiding in the love of God can true union with Him be realized. In verse 8 the matter of our exercising love, as the outcome of God's love experienced by us, was put negatively, "He that loveth not knoweth not God"; here it is put positively, "He that abideth in love abideth in God, and God abideth in Him." Each of these statements "God is love" is connected with the fact that He "sent His Son into the world" (verses 9 and 14); the former followed the first statement that "God is love", the latter precedes the repetition. In each case the sending of His Son is a proof of God's love, and the out-working of that love in us, in the exercise of love one to another, constitutes the great sign of the abiding presence of God within us and of our abiding in Him. That holy intimacy is the blessed experience of all true children of God.

VERSE 17. **Herein is love made perfect with us, that we may have**

boldness in the day of judgment; because as He is, even so are we in this world.—From this verse to the end of the chapter the Apostle enlarges upon the experience, mentioned in verse 16, that is to say, with regard both to our knowledge of God and His nature, and the enjoyment of the most intimate communion with Him, and the practical communion with Him, and the practical effect of this knowledge and faith as manifested in our own exercise of love.

The opening statement of verse 17 may be rendered as follows: "In this is love (*i.e.*, the Divine love) perfected in us." The "herein" connects the preceding verse with what follows. When God sees the perfecting of His love in us, as shown in our love to others, that is to say, when He sees us united to Him, not only positionally but in practical experience, He sees in us the likeness of His own Son, the One in whom He is well pleased; and in this way "as He is, even so are we in this world." This last statement has to do with the character of Christ, not with the fact that we are saved because of our identification with Christ.

Now this manifestation of Christ's nature in us is connected with our boldness in the day of judgment, that is, the boldness with which we shall stand before the Judgment-seat of Christ. The ground of this boldness is our present likeness to Him. Not the matter of our being acquitted, or cleared of guilt, and so standing without condemnation before God, is here in view, but the assurance that, in as far as we manifest the Divine nature in our love to others, we shall stand blameless, without reproach and without regret, before Christ's Judgment-seat. The phrase "the Day of Judgment" has the article before each noun in the original, and nowhere else occurs exactly like this. Thus it is to be distinguished from the phrase without the articles, as in Matt. 10: 15; 11: 22, 24; 12: 36; 2 Pet. 2: 9; 3: 7. The Judgment-seat of Christ is to be distinguished from the Day of Judgment of the ungodly, which is entirely another and subsequent event.

VERSE 18. **There is no fear in love: but perfect love casteth out fear, because fear hath punishment;**—This gives a proof, by way of a general statement of fact, of what was stated in the preceding verse as to our having boldness in the Day of Judgment because love is made perfect in us. In other words, that must be so because of the impossibility of the co-existence of love and fear in the way here mentioned. Fear is expelled by perfect love, and love is prevented by fear from being perfected.

This verse does not intimate that fear and love cannot exist in the same person; for they obviously do. The point is that, where God's love is being perfected in us, it gives no room for fear; not, again, the fear of God in which we are to walk, a fear lest we should grieve Him, but the fear of meeting with His reprobation. The former fear should characterize us, but, as to the latter, we should so live that it is absent from us. If we are not manifesting love, we have cause for fear that, instead of having boldness at the Judgment-seat of Christ, we shall lose our reward, the expression of His approval.

The word rendered "punishment" also means "chastisement." It does not convey the idea of torment, as in the A.V.; it suggests the immediate consequence of the sense of sin.

and he that feareth is not made perfect in love.—As long as anyone is in fear of judgment, he makes clear thereby that he is not perfected in love (see verse 17). Punishment, then, in the sense of the word here indicated, is a token of imperfection. Perfect love leaves nothing to be feared (see Rom. 8: 15). The fear which has punishment is not a holy awe, characteristic of filial piety, but that slavish fear, which is banished by perfect love.

The present participle rendered "he that feareth" expresses a habitual state, the state which is the very negation of the enjoyment of love; love which is the fulfilling of the Law (Rom. 13: 10) leaves nothing to be feared.

VERSE 19. **We love, because He first loved us.**—The "Him" of the A.V. is not in the most authentic MSS. It was introduced as a result of a misapprehension. The Apostle is not here speaking of our showing love to God in response to His love to us; his point is that no exercise of Christian love on our part is possible apart from God's love to us. This is borne out by the verses which follow.

There is stress on both the pronouns "we" and "He." The word "first" also bears emphasis, and serves to point the connection with the preceding verses. Fear finds no place in the one in whom the love of God is perfected; the incompatibility of the two is due to the fact that God is the Source of love; the exercise of it on our part is not only the outcome of His but thereby carries with it the freedom from apprehensiveness that we are not pleasing God.

VERSE 20. **If a man say, I love God, and hateth his brother, he is a liar:**—For the phrase "If a man say" see 1: 6, 8, 10; 2: 4, 6, 9, etc. It is plainly characteristic of this Epistle, and is indicative of the many evil conditions and influences which were at work, to the detriment of the spiritual life of believers. Against this mere professionalism they were to be on their guard, and particularly the profession here mentioned, of showing love to God while denying it to our brother. There is a close connection between this verse and what precedes. If we refrain from showing love to our brother, however much we may know of the doctrine of love to God, there is no real comprehension or appreciation of it, because there is no reponse on our part to His love (verse 19). Whatever freedom from fear there is in such a case, is mere presumption, its absence not being due to the expulsive power of perfect love (verse 18). Such a person is a liar, and his character bears no resemblance to that of God. He neither knows the nature of God, nor does he enjoy communion with Him (verse 16). He does not know God (verse 8) nor has he been born of Him (verse 7). His spirit is not the Spirit of truth but the spirit of error (verse 6).

for he that loveth not his brother whom he hath seen, cannot love God whom he hath not seen.—As in 3: 14, 15, not to love one's brother is spoken of as the same as hating.

The perfect tense "hath seen" expresses an abiding condition. The brother is viewed not as one simply whom we can see but as one who is constantly before our eyes.

While it is true that, if a man fails to discharge his duty in regard to things he sees, he is not likely to do so in regard to what he does not see, yet more than that is suggested here. It is not simply that what is invisible is more difficult to love than what is visible, but that the absence of practical love to one's brother in the material circumstances of every-day life rules out the possibility of love to God; that is essentially a matter of faith, as being exercised towards Him Who is invisible. There is a connection between this verse and what is said of the invisibility of God in verse 12.

VERSE 21. **And this commandment have we from Him, that he who loveth God love his brother also.**—In this verse what has been regarded as spiritually inevitable in the preceding verse, is put as a distinct command. Not only is love to God impossible where we do not love our brother, but love to our brother is binding upon us; cp. Lev. 19: 18; Deut. 6: 5; Luke 10: 27; Rom. 13: 9, 10; Gal. 5: 14; and see John 13: 34, 35 and chaps. 2, 3, 4 of this Epistle. The "Him" seems clearly to be God.

CHAPTER V

ANALYSIS OF CHAPTER V

(A) VERSES 1-12—FAITH AS THE SOURCE OF THE LIFE OF LOVE

(B) VERSES 13-17—THE LIFE OF FAITH IN RELATION TO PRAYER

(C) VERSES 18-21—THE ASSURED FACTS CONCERNING THE LIFE ETERNAL

(A) Verses 1-12

	Verses
(1) Faith and its Effects:	1-5
(a) In regard to fellow-believers:	1-3
1. The subject of faith—Jesus as the Christ	1a
2. Faith the evidence of the new birth	1b
3. The effect of faith—love:	<u>10-3</u>
(i) Love to God	
(ii) Love to God's children:	
The assurance of (ii)	2
The ground of the assurance:	
(1) Love to God	
(2) Obedience to His commandments	
The essence of (i)	3
(1) Obedience to His commandments	
(2) The character of His commandments	
(b) In regard to the world:	4, 5
1. The person who overcomes—(first description) born of God	4a
2. What he overcomes—the world	4b
3. The means of overcoming—faith	4c
4. The person who overcomes—(second description) he who believes that Jesus is the Son of God	5

Verses

(c) Special Prayer (in accordance with brotherly love):   16

   1. The exigency   16a

     (i) The occasion—a brother sinning not unto death

     (ii) The object—the preservation of his spiritual life

   2. The exception: 16b

     (i) The occasion—sin unto death

     (ii) The restriction—no exhortation to pray

   3. The explanation: 17

     (i) The nature of sin

     (ii) The discinction confirmed

(C)   Verses 18–21

(4) The Assured Facts concerning the Life Eternal: 18–21

  (a) The first assurance (the maintenance of the life):   18

    1. The evidence of one born of God—he does not go on in sin

    2. The keeping power—the Only-Begotten One keepeth him

    3. The security—the evil one toucheth him not

  (b) The second assurance (the origin of the life):   19

    1. The source—believers are of God

    2. The contrast—the state of the world

  (c) The third assurance (the Person in Whom the life consists):   20

    1. The First Advent of the Son

    2. The gift received from the Son:

     (i) The purpose of the gift

     (ii) The assurance of life in the Father and in the Son

    3. The Deity of the Son

    4. The Son as the essence and the embodiment of the life

  (d) The closing command against what is detrimental to the life: 21

    1. The appeal to the readers as little children

    2. The command to keep from idols

Chapter V.   (A)   Verses 1-12

Introductory Note

This chapter has two parts, verses 1-12, verses 13-21. The former belongs to the central division of the Epistle which comes under the heading "God is love." The last part forms the conclusion of the Epistle and deals especially with the truth that God is love. Verses 1-12 deal especially with faith, and with the subject of faith witness is connected as being the basis of faith. Hence the various witnesses which form the foundation of the believer's faith are dealt with in this passage, but, first of all, faith worketh by love, and as the Apostle has been dealing with the exercise of love he continues this now in connection with the subject of faith.

VERSE 1.   **Whosoever believeth**—Lit., "everyone that believeth", "every believer." For a similar construction see 2: 29; 3: 3, 4; 4: 2, 3, 7. The words "believe" and "faith" occur for the first time in the Epistle in this passage, and are connected with the subject of love, with which the Apostle is dealing; see the Introductory Note above.

that Jesus is the Christ—What is involved in this is not merely the existence of a historical fact; to believe that Jesus is the Christ, is to believe in the personal manifestation of God Himself, and, further this involves the foundation truths of the faith relating to Christ. The acceptance of the doctrine leads to the acceptance of the Person.

is begotten of God:—Perfect tense, "has been begotten." See John 1: 12, 13; 3: 2-8; Jas. 1: 18; 1 Pte. 1: 3.

and whosoever loveth Him that begat loveth him also that is begotten of Him.—This puts verse 1 into close connection with what has preceded. Since every believer has part in the gift of Divine life, by which he is born of God, it is inevitable that this life will be manifested in love to those who likewise are born of God. This involves both what has been already stated, as to the recognition that Jesus is the Christ, and what has been set forth in chapter 4. In chapter 4: 15 the Apostle spoke of the confession that Jesus is the Son of God; here he speaks of the belief which lies behind the confession. That is to say, in the former passage he puts stress upon the outward expression, here upon the inward basis, of the believer's life. In chapter 4 stress was laid upon the outward expression of brotherly love, as the effect of the inward experience of the love of God; here the stress is laid upon the outward expression, as the effect of the inward experience of the new birth. In the former passage the truth set forth was that every believer has experience of God's love and therefore shows it in love to others. Here what is set forth is that every believer shares the gift of life in Christ, and this again involves the manifestation of love to those who likewise are blessed. None of this is possible apart from faith in Christ, but, on the other hand, faith inevitably leads to the exercise of love. The whole of this passage teaches, not that in loving our brother we rise to the love of God, but that, on the contrary, God Himself is the source of all the love that we can and do show.

VERSE 2. **Hereby we know**—*Ginōskō*, we have the constant experience of knowing.

that we love the children of God, when we love God, and do His commandments.—What was stated in 4: 20, 21, is purposely put in the opposite way in this verse. In the former passage love to God is the fulfilment of His commandments, which are shown to have their evidence in the love of His children. This same truth is stressed by being put in the converse way in the present passage. In other words, if we want to know whether we love our brother, it is necessary to ask if we love God, for the motive cause of love lies in God Himself, for "God is love." Here the test of our love to God is the doing of His commandments, that is to say, in loving our neighbour. Taken together, then, the two passages show that love to God and love to one another are essentially associated and mutually evidential.

The word rendered "when" occurs nowhere else in John's Epistles; it signifies "whensoever." That is to say, the constant realisation of loving God and doing His commandments involves the practical experience of loving the children of God.

VERSE 3. **For this is the love of God, that we keep His commandments:**—God's commandments, being the expression of His love, are designed to keep us in the element of His love. The fulfilment of His commandments by us is the revelation of His character through our instrumentality. His commandments make known His nature, and we show His nature when we keep them (cp. 4: 8, 16).

and His commandments are not grievous.—The word *barus* signifies burdensome. The statement does not mean this, that God's commandments are not difficult to keep, it means that they do not impose a burden when they are kept. In the keeping of them there is great reward (Psa. 19: 11). "My yoke is easy, and My burden is light" (Matt. 11: 30). What imposes a burden is disobedience to His will. The more we fulfil it the happier we are. For it is then that His love is perfected in us and casts out fear (4: 18). How different the requirements and restrictions laid down by the Pharisees, "burdens grievous to be borne"! The Lord supplies strength for the fulfilment of His commandments, His love makes them light, and He rewards the doing of it.

VERSE 4. **For whatsoever is begotten of God overcometh the world:**—This provides the reason why keeping God's commandments, and so exercising love, is not a burden grievous to be borne. The reason stated brings before us the character of the world; the spirit of the world is opposed to the fulfilment of the commandments of God. To do His commandments, therefore, is to overcome the spirit of the world. The doing of His commandments is possible only to one who is born of God, and the power to carry them out comes, not from self, but from Him.

A deep significance attaches to the collective neuter "whatsoever." Firstly, it serves to give less prominence to the person who overcomes and to indicate rather the power which is impaired to him in virtue of his new birth. Secondly, it serves to make the statement more comprehensive, by reason of what has just been said, as not merely persons are in view but the power that introduces them.

As in verse 1, the original has the perfect tense, "has been begotten" and this stresses the permanent effect of the spiritual birth, namely, a lasting power for victory over the world.

and this is the victory that hath overcome the world, even our faith.— The verb rendered "hath overcome" is in the aorist, or point, tense, and this takes us back to the beginning of the life, for the power for victory came when faith first began to be exercised, that is to say, when we received Christ by faith and were born of God. For then we passed spiritually out of the sphere of the world into union with Christ. The unregenerate person is not governed by the Spirit of God. Faith not merely brings to us the new birth, but with it the power to overcome the opposition of the spirit that characterizes the world. The victory which was thus gained by faith, the proving of things not seen, brought us into a life which was designed to be characterized by victorious power.

The word *nikē*, "victory", occurs here only in the New Testament. The noun "faith" is nowhere else found in John's Epistles and Gospel, though the subject of believing is prominent throughout.

VERSE 5. **And who is he that overcometh the world,**—The article with the present participle, translated "he that overcometh", is practically equivalent to a noun, "the overcomer." As in 2: 22, the article does not define a particular person but represents what is true of every such person.

but he that believeth that Jesus is the Son of God?—This verse continues the theme of verse 4, and expresses the particular point in regard to which the faith that brings the new birth and overcomes the world is exercised, namely, that Jesus is the Son of God. The exercise of faith, however, is not the barren acceptance of a fact. The faith that makes a person the child of God is never simply a belief of something about Jesus, for the Person Himself is always presented as the object of faith and this involves the reception of Christ Himself by faith as the One set forth by the truth about Him. Hence the comprehensive character of the acknowledgement that Jesus is the Son of God. This involves, for instance, the great truths of the pre-existent Sonship of Christ, His Incarnation, and the fulfilment thereby of all that the Name "Jesus" means.

Such faith, then, brings to one who exercises it, a power to overcome in him all that is characteristic of the world. It brings into his life, for example, the means of loving as God loves, in contrast to the spirit of selfishness and strife that is in the world.

In the next part of the chapter the Apostle expands the subject of the basis upon which faith rests, namely, some of the great truths relating to the Person of Christ and the witness given concerning Him. See the Analysis of Chapter 5.

VERSE 6. **This is he**—That is, Jesus the Son of God, as mentioned in the last verse, conveying the truth that the eternal Son of God is one and the same Person with the historic Jesus, a truth which, the Apostle shows, receives the greatest possible witness.

that came by water and blood, even Jesus Christ; not with the water only, but with the water and with the blood.—Of the numerous attempts to explain this passage only two call for consideration here, namely, that the reference is (1) to the water and blood that flowed from Christ's pierced side, (2) to Christ's baptism in Jordan and His death upon the Cross in the shedding of His blood.

The first of these two explanations has regard to the record in John 19: 34, the water and blood which flowed from the side of Christ representing that which meets our double need. Some regard the water as setting forth the means of the cleansing of the sinner from his sin and the blood as setting forth that by which his sins are atoned for. In addition to this, however, the context points to life as the subject of the Apostle's teaching here. With this in view the water would indicate the life imparted through the cleansing of sin on the ground of the death of Christ. The leper needed not only the application of the blood of sacrifice (Lev. 14: 14) but he was required to bathe his flesh in water, symbolizing cleansing and life (see verse 5, "living water," and cp. John 7: 38). Life is imparted and maintained by the living Christ on the ground of His death. The blood, standing for the death of Christ in the shedding of His blood, is the ground upon which God justifies the believing sinner. But the blood and the water were applied not only to the leper but to Aaron and his sons, who represent believers in their priestly capacity (Ex. 29 and Lev. 8), for the life is bestowed that it may be lived to God.

In view of the statement in verse 11, that the combined witness of the Spirit, the water and the blood is this, "that God gave unto us eternal life and this life is in His Son", it seems necessary to bear in mind that the blood signifies the basis upon which life is bestowed as well as righteousness reckoned. Lev. 17: 11 states firstly that the life of the flesh is in the blood; secondly that it has been given by God to make atonement; thirdly, that "it is the blood that maketh atonement, by reason of the life" (R.V.). Sin has forfeited the life. In order, therefore, that life should be imparted to the sinner a substitutionary death was necessary by the shedding of the blood of a sinless Person so that sin might be covered and removed. "Christ died for our sins" (1 Cor. 15: 3); He "gave Himself up" for us (Gal. 2: 20). In the removal thereby of sin, righteousness being reckoned to the believing sinner, he also receives the gift of life.

The change of preposition in the verse is significant. In the statement "This is He that came by water and blood," the preposition is *dia*, "by means of"; that preposition is simply instrumental. In the statement which follows, "not with the water only, but with the water and with the blood," the preposition is *en*, which means both "by" and "in"; that is to say, while it is still instrumental, it gives the additional idea of the element in which the purpose of the Lord's mission was accomplished. Accordingly, as *en* is the more comprehensive preposition it is repeated in each case emphatically with the mention of the water and the blood.

Those who hold the other view consider that the Apostle is still combating the false teachings of the Gnostics, who taught that at His baptism the Divine *Logos* united Himself with the man Jesus. They denied that the Divine Person had part in what was effected in the shedding of His blood, since the *Logos*, they said, departed from Jesus at Gethsemane.

The former explanation seems to be the right one.

VERSE 7. **And it is the Spirit that beareth witness, because the Spirit is the truth.**—That is to say, the Holy Spirit; see 3: 24; 4: 13. "That beareth witness" translates the article with the participle, which is virtually a noun "the Witness-Bearer." So in John 6: 63, "the Spirit is the Life-Giver."

The threefold witness is about to be given (see verse 8), but, as a preliminary to this, the Person of the Holy Spirit is mentioned first alone, as being in the Godhead. The Spirit of God bears witness by His operation in the heart concerning the Person and Work of Christ. On the day of Pentecost and subsequently He bore witness through the Apostles and others. He bears witness through the Holy Scriptures, which are God-breathed (2 Tim. 3: 16), and through testimony in accordance with them the Scriptures constitute the truth because "the Spirit is the truth."

The Apostle conveys through this latter statement the Deity of the Holy Spirit. "God is true" (Psa. 31: 5). Christ is "the truth" (John 14: 16), and "the Spirit is the truth." He is one in Divine nature with the Father and the Son.

The special witness to which this passage refers is the identity of Jesus with the Son of God, and to this great fact the Spirit of truth bears witness. See John 14: 26 and 15: 26.

The alternative rendering "it is the Spirit that beareth witness that the Spirit is the truth" is possible, but is not borne out by the context.

Note on verse 7 in the A.V.

The 7th verse, given in the A.V. is not part of the original. No Greek manuscript earlier than the 14th century contains the passage. No version earlier than the 5th century in any other language contains it.

Only Latin versions contain it previous to the 14th century. None of the Greek or Latin "Fathers" in all their testimonies in the first four and a half centuries about the Trinity, quote the passage. Again what the passage states about the witness in heaven is not confirmed by any other passage in Scripture. Moreover, the statement makes a break into the sense of the whole passage. It must, therefore, be regarded as an interpolation by some copyist.

VERSE 8. **For there are three who bear witness,**—The present continuous tense indicates the permanency of the witness.

the Spirit, and the water, and the blood:—The triple witness is a witness concerning life (see verse 11, R.V., which is to be connected immediately with this verse). The Spirit of God applies to the believer's heart the realization of the efficacy of the blood of Christ and the ministry of what is set forth by the water. All this constitutes a ministry of life, and what has been said above as to the cleansing of the leper (Lev. 14), and the preparation of the priests for their service (Ex. 28 and Lev. 8), has to do with the bestowel of life through cleansing, on the one hand (for the leper, instead of living and dying apart, could come into the camp), and, on the other hand, of a life of service to God. In each case water and blood and oil were applied, the oil being emblematic of the Holy Spirit.

and the three agree in one.—Lit., 'and the three are unto (or into) one.' They are united in one witness and have one object and effect. For the point of the witness and its effects see verses 11 and 12. The special phrase "into one" with the article occurs here only in the N.T.

VERSE 9. **If we receive the witness of men, the witness of God is greater:**—The "If" simply introduces what is an acknowledged fact, not a matter of doubt. That is to say "if we receive the witness of men, and it is an acknowledged fact that we do. . . ."

The sense of the word "receive" is "to accept as valid." If we are accustomed to accept a testimony in regard to earthly facts, how much more shall we rely confidently upon the Divine testimony! For a similar argument see the Lord's words in John 8: 17. In the present passage the argument is *a fortiori.*

for the witness of God is this that He hath borne witness concerning His Son.—The word "for" is, more literally, "because." The statement lays stress on the fact that the witness is not merely concerning a Person named Jesus, but that it is a witness concerning Him as the Son of God. The perfect tense "hath borne witness" expresses the abiding effects of the witness given. (See recapitulatory note after verse 1).

VERSE 10. **He that believeth on the Son of God hath the witness in him:**—This verse expands verse 5. The present continuous tense, "he that believeth", expresses the habitual attitude of faith. This is the first time in this Epistle where the verb "to believe" is followed by the preposition *eis*, which, in this construction, combines the thoughts of the direction in which faith is exercised and the rest it reposes on its object. Faith thus exercised involves the fullest trust in, and reliance upon, a person. The construction is found some 40 times in the Gospel of John.

The title "Son of God" is used here as being the great point of the Apostle's subject. For other passages concerning the witness of the Spirit in our hearts, cp. Rom. 8: 16; Gal. 4: 6. The one who accepts the witness of God and believes on His Son has the continual witness internally.

he that believeth not God hath made Him a liar; because he hath not believed in the witness that God hath borne concerning His Son.—Not only are the believer and the unbeliever set in contrast in this verse, but the effects of belief and unbelief, the happy experiences of faith and the solemn effect of unbelief. These contrasting effects are stressed, rather than the condition upon which the witness is given. Since the witness concerning His Son has been given by God, not to accept it is to impute falsehood to Him.

Here again the preposition *eis* is used after "to believe". The phrase "to believe in the witness" occurs nowhere else in the N.T. Elsewhere it is simply "to believe the witness." The same phrase is used here with reference both to Christ and to the witness God has given. That is to say, the Person and the truth about Him are inseparable.

It is well here to recapitulate the line of teaching thus far in the whole of this chapter.

In the first three verses the subject passes from that of love to that of obedience, and in the next two verses to conflict and victory, the necessary condition for which is faith. Now faith brings to the believer the power of the Holy Spirit, in applying to his heart the effects of the death of Christ, and in giving him, as an inward witness, the consciousness of that power. Further, the consciousness arising from the witness comes from God, and it is a witness concerning His Son. There are four points to be noticed here particularly: firstly, the witness comes from God; secondly, it is concerning His Son and His mission, His death and resurrection; thirdly, the witness is threefold, that of the Spirit, the water and the blood; fourthly, it is a witness concerning life in Christ as His Son. Such a witness commands our faith, which therefore rests upon an absolutely reliable basis. Accordingly, faith is the effect of the witness, and is spoken of as the habitual attitude of the soul. Again, the witness is an abiding possession which glorifies God. In contrast with this, the unbeliever, who deliberately refuses the testimony that God has given, makes Him a liar (verse 10).

VERSE 11. **And the witness is this,**—The variety of rendering in the A.V., of the one word in the original, by which, instead of keeping to the word "witness," a change is made to the word "record," tends to mar the translation, especially as "record" has a different meaning in English. The R.V. rightly adheres to the one word throughout.

that God gave unto us eternal life, and this life is in His Son.—This verse and the next bring us to the climax of the whole passage and gather up much of what has been set forth in the Epistle from its commencement. At the outset the Apostle stated that his subject was the Word of life, of whom he and his fellow-Apostles had had personal experience. Then, after leading his readers through the subjects of light and life, he has shown how faith, working by love, imparts power to a life in which love is manifested, giving victory over opposition. He has further shown how God has borne witness concerning His Son, and how His life becomes ours. Now, summing up his subject, he shows how the possession of eternal life involves the possession of the Son of God Himself, without whom eternal life is impossible.

The aorist tense, "gave," marks more distinctly the giving as a definite act, stressing the greatness of the act rather than the abiding results, which have been elsewhere stressed in the Epistle. With the fact that the Son of God, who is the embodiment of life, is also the Source thereof, cp. John 1: 4; 5: 26; Acts 3: 15.

VERSE 12. **He that hath the Son hath the life; he that hath not the Son of God hath not the life.**—This is a statement arising from what has been mentioned in the preceding verse as the witness. As in 2: 23, to confess the Son is to have the Father, and to deny the Son is not to have the Father, so here, to have the Son is to possess the life that is essentially His, and not to possess Him is not to possess the life. The parallel between the two verses is significant. That the full title, "the Son of God," is given in the second part of the verse and not in the first, indicates that, with regard to the first part and those who have the Son, they know that He is the Son of God, and such believers do not need to be reminded of this; whereas those who do not possess the Son need the reminder as to what Person it is whom their unbelief refuses.

The order in the two parts of the verse, in regard to the possession of life, is different. In the first part the words "the life" bear stress (*i.e.*, it is the possession of life that is involved in the possession of the Son); in the last statement of the verse the word "hath" bears stress (he is destitute of life who has not the Son). The two statements, with their contrast in emphasis, strikingly sum up all that the Apostle has set forth as to the distinction between the believer and the unbeliever, the regenerate and the unregenerate, the children of God and the children of the Evil One.

(B)   Verses 13–17

Introductory Note

In the thirteenth verse stress is laid upon the fact that the readers are those who believe on the name of the Son of God and have eternal life, and this follows the distinction made in the preceding verse and likewise connects this passage with verse 5. The Apostle at the same time expresses the purpose of his Epistle, namely to, confirm his readers in the assurance of their possession. He then shows what the possession of life involves in regard to boldness towards God, to prayer and intercession, and the restoration of an erring brother. This leads to the conclusion of the Epistle, in which are specified the assurances which believers possess and which involve the great fundamental principles of the Epistle itself.

VERSE 13. **These things have I written unto you.**—The word rendered "have written", is the epistolary use of the past tense. The Greeks worded a letter from the point of view of the time when the recipient would be reading it. In English we should say "I am writing," unless we had come to the end of a letter, when we might say, "I have written." Either would be accurate in the present verse. The Apostle is referring to the whole of his Epistle.

that ye may know—Not now a matter of progressive knowledge (*ginōskō*), but the assurance of intuitive knowledge (*oida*).

that ye have eternal life,—The object for which the Apostle wrote the Gospel was that his readers might "believe that Jesus is the

Christ, the Son of God", and that believing they might "have life in His Name" (20: 31). His object in the Epistle is that they may know that they have eternal life. The Gospel was written to produce faith and its effects, the Epistle was written to confirm faith. The Gospel was written that the blessing of eternal life might be obtained; the Epistle, to produce the joy that comes from possession (1: 4), the joy of fellowship with God and with His Son and with fellow-saints. Stress is upon the word "eternal." Faith does not produce in the believer a transient emotion of enthusiasm, nor does it bring him under a passing influence; it introduces him to a life of union and fellowship with Christ in its fixed and unchangeable character. Faith is not merely an acquiescence in certain facts, but the means of permanent relationship with Him who is the very source of life.

even unto you that believe on the name of the Son of God.—This clause is put in the position of emphasis, at the end of the verse, and sets believers in renewed contrast to those who, being unbelievers, have not eternal life. The R.V. follows the most authentic MSS. here.

In 3: 23 (the only other place in this Epistle where the expression "the name" occurs) the Apostle spoke of believing "the name" (R.V. margin). Here the phrase is "believe on the name," lit., believe "into the name", expressive of the union produced by believing. In 3: 23 the title was "His Son Jesus Christ" (see notes there); here it is "the Son of God", as in the context above (vv. 8–12).

VERSE 14. **And this is the boldness which we have toward Him,—** For a similar style of statement see 1: 5; 2: 25; 3: 11; 4: 23; 5: 3, 4, 6, 9, 11, 20.

This verse leads up to an exhortation as to intercessory prayer, especially on behalf of an erring brother. The subject of boldness has been mentioned in three parts of this Epistle already, (1) in 2: 28, in connection with freedom from shame at the Judgment-seat of Christ; (2) in 3: 21, in connection with the possession of a clear conscience towards God; (3) in 4: 17, as the outcome of the perfecting of God's love in us and of our likeness to Christ. In this passage (4) boldness is the basis of our confidence in prayer.

that, if we ask anything according to His will, He heareth us:—The word rendered "ask" is *aiteō*; it is here used in the Middle Voice, signifying that the petitioner has a more special interest in the matter of his request than the Active Voice would imply. For the difference between this word and *erōtaō*, see notes on verse 16 below.

Since the will of God for His children has as its design their greatest possible benefit, it is only Divine grace that puts the stated limitation upon the fulfilment of our request. If our prayer has as its object, not our self-interest, but our brother's real good, the condition is fulfilled and prayer will be answered in God's time and way. For the other condition laid down in this Epistle in regard to answers to prayer, see 3: 22. The two passages are very similar in this respect. For if we keep God's commandments and do what is pleasing in His sight (3: 22), our actions evince an attitude of heart that is consistent with the will of God.

VERSE 15.   **and if we know**—*Oida*, as in verse 13, where see note.

that He heareth us whatsoever we ask, we know that we have the petitions which we have asked of Him.—In this verse the first occurrence of the word "ask" is still in the Middle Voice (see above). The second, which is in the perfect tense, is in the Active Voice. The change from the one voice to the other does not indicate any lessening of the interest which the petitioner has in making the request, it serves to bring into still greater prominence the Person who grants the petition, and this is borne out by the addition "of Him" (lit., "from Him"). Simply as a sentence it would be complete if it ended at the word "asked."

This statement presupposes that the condition mentioned in verse 14 is fulfilled. In other words, on the ground that our union with Christ gives us boldness towards God, and that our will is subject to His will, we have the assurance that the petitions, presented in the spirit of unselfishness and submission, have already been granted.

VERSE 16.   **If any man see his brother sinning a sin not unto death,**—This provides an instance of the unselfish motive in prayer that seeks the real welfare of a brother. Such prayer is the outcome of the indwelling of Christ in the heart, and the perfecting of His love, as mentioned in 4: 17, 18.

Judging from the general tenor of the Epistle, and its special subject of the family of God, the word "brother" refers to a brother in the Lord. Indeed, the reference could not be to the unconverted, for such a one is already in death. The phrase "sinning a sin", while necessarily referring to an act, is suggestive rather of the condition that leads to it, and the Epistle, where speaking of an act, not infrequently points to the state which produces it.

The phrase "unto death" signifies "tending towards death", rather than the actual condition of being in death. Accordingly, this would seem to rule out the view that the state referred to is that in which a child of God has lost all communion with the Lord, for that would involve a condition of spiritual death already experienced, instead of that which tends towards it.

As to the subject of death, the only conclusion that seems possible is that the reference is to physical death. That is spoken of as the result of certain sins, as in the case of Ananias and Sapphira, and that of the moral delinquent in 1 Cor. 5, and again in the case of those who partake of the Lord's Supper unworthily (1 Cor. 11: 30, where sleep refers to physical death).

he shall ask, and God shall give him life for them that sin not unto death.—The word rendered "ask" is again *aiteō*, and is in the Active Voice (see notes above). The future tense does not imply either a command or what will probably take place, it rather suggests that, since the subject itself is prayer, and the one who is praying is looked upon as being in harmony with the will of God, the asking on his part is a foregone conclusion, and will produce the result stated.

As to the "him", the R.V. text seems to give the accurate meaning, namely, that God is the Giver, and that the "him" refers to the petitioner. The prayer of faith saves the sick (Jas. 5: 15) and therefore we are exhorted to pray for such cases as are mentioned in the first part of verse 16, so that the life of the erring one may be spared, God fulfilling the request in the case of those who sin not unto death. This meaning seems to be more probable than the suggestion that "him" is the erring one himself, on whose behalf the prayer is offered. The change to the plural, "them that sin", simply makes the statement more general; for sinning "not unto death" is not likely to be confined to one case.

There is a sin unto death:—Probably the R.V. margin is here to be preferred, "there is sin unto death." This would indicate not some particular act of sin but rather the state or condition of sin producing acts. In the cases of the persons referred to in the preceding note on "unto death", there was a sinful state of heart which produced the results mentioned.

not concerning this do I say that he should make request.—There is stress on the word "this", which refers to "sin unto death." The verb rendered "make request" is *erōtaō*, in distinction from *aiteō* "to ask." In the preceding part of the verse, and in verses 14, 15, the distinction is that *aiteō* implies a more humble supplication than *erōtaō*. *Erōtaō* suggests the more familiar request of one who is enjoying ready access to, and constant communion with, God. The change of verb perhaps indicates that, while certainly the appeal of holy intimacy (suggested by the word "request") is not advisable, much less would it be advisable for the still more humble and urgent supplication to be made. Accordingly, in the case of "sin not unto death" we may intercede with the assurance that our prayer is heard, but in the case of "sin unto death" we must leave the matter with God, at the same time refraining from anything like censoriousness or criticism.

While a distinction is given between two kinds of sin, yet the passage affords no specification or criterion by means of which one might be drawn to pass judgment or proceed to tabulate sins under the two headings.

VERSE 17. **All unrighteousness is sin:**—*Adikia*, "unrighteousness", signifies that which is contrary to what is right. Contrast 3: 4, where sin was defined as lawlessness, *i.e.*, setting law aside. The present verse does not give a definition of sin, it deals with the principle underlying it, whereas the statement in 3: 4 declares the character of sin. In both cases the Apostle is striking a blow against the teachings of the Gnostics, that what would be sin in ordinary cases is not sin for enlightened people.

and there is a sin not unto death.—Or rather as before "sin not unto death." The restatement of this indicates a suggestion that there is abundant scope for intercessory prayer, that there are plenty of cases demanding it, and that, with the exception mentioned in verse 15, any act of unrighteousness is an occasion for intercession. This verse combines a warning against unrighteousness on the part of each one of us, with an intimation of the need of that tender-heartedness regarding the wrong acts of others which leads to intercession for them.

(C)   Verses 18–21

Introductory Note

From this verse to the end of the chapter the Apostle declares three things which are recognized by the conscience of believers, while, in bringing his Epistle to a close, he recalls much of what he has written before. The first of the three things is, that there is a power at the disposal of the believer enabling him to keep from sin (cp. 2: 1,

14, 20; 3: 6, 9; 4: 13; 5: 4). The second is, that this power is consequent upon the new birth, and is realized in separation from the world (cp. 2: 29; 3: 9; 5: 4, 5). The third is, that, by reason of the new birth, we have an anointing from God and an abiding relationship with the Father and with the Son (cp. 2: 3, 27; 3: 2, 24; 4: 7, 12, 15, 16). The first of the three has to do with our relationship to Christ.

VERSE 18. We know—*Oida*, "we have an intuitive knowledge", Divinely imparted. This word, expressive of the confident certitude begotten of faith, likewise begins verses 19 and 20, and links them together in the way mentioned in the Introductory Note just given. At the same time it is obviously designed as against the boasted and spurious "knowledge" of the Gnostics.

that whosoever is begotten of God—More lit., "whosoever has been begotten", expressive of the abiding effect of the Divine operations in the case of the believer. The rendering "begotten" should be used in both parts of the verse (not as in the A.V.).

sinneth not;—This is in the present continuous tense, and recalls 3: 9, where the A.V. "commit" gives a wrong impression, as if speaking of an act instead of a series of acts or a course of sin. The Apostle is not now speaking of sin unto death, but, as in chapter 3, of a continuous course of sin, which is entirely incompatible with the new birth. In other words, he leaves the subject of the sin which is possible and calls for intercession, and that which does not, and resumes, for final mention, the subject of that state of sin which, in the case of a believer, yields to the power that makes for repentance and restoration.

but he that was begotten of God keepeth him,—The change of tense, "was begotten", is noticeable. Whereas the perfect tense, "he that hath been begotten", refers to the believer as a child of God, in contrast to those who have not become so, the aorist or point tense, "was begotten", points to a fact in the past and refers to the Son of God, "the Only-Begotten from the Father" (John 1: 14), in contrast to the evil one. Christ is the Keeper (cp. John 17: 12). The rendering "him" (not "himself") is supported by weighty MS. evidence and is in keeping with the context.

and the evil one toucheth him not.—The word rendered *haptomai*, "toucheth", here signifies "to lay hold of." The evil one assaults, but he cannot sever the vital connection between the believer and Christ. However grievously a child of God may sin, he can never be snatched out of the hand, either of Christ or of the Father (John 10: 28, 29). *Haptomai* is to be distinguished from *thigganō*, which means simply "to touch", as in Heb. 11: 28; 12:20.

VERSE 19.   **We know that we are of God,**—For "we know" see at the beginning of verse 18. This statement has its basis in what is said in verse 18. That we are of God (*ek*, "out of", in the sense of "from", *i.e.*, as to the source of our spiritual relationship) means that we have been begotten by Him; we owe to Him and His power the fact that we are His children.

and the whole world lieth in the evil one.—This is also what "we know"; it is not a fact independent of the knowledge of the children of God. There is stress upon "the whole", and this may be brought out by the rendering "the world, the whole of it."

There is again a connection with verse 18. While believers are beyond the power of the evil one to separate them from Christ, the rest of mankind, who constitute "the world", are in his power (see John 12: 31; 14: 30; 16: 11); they are controlled by him as "the prince of this world", and their condition is therefore that of spiritual death (contrast the next verse).

The separation which exists between Christ and the evil one should find its counterpart in the separation of the believer from the world.

The A.V. "wickedness" is inconsistent with the fact that everywhere else in this Epistle the phrase is necessarily "the evil one" (2: 13; 2: 14; 3: 12; 5: 18).

There is no contradiction between this verse and what is said in 2: 2; for the propitiation made by Christ for the world was provisional and potential; it becomes actual only through faith.

VERSE 20.   **And we know that the Son of God is come,**—This introduces the third fact in the series of certitudes intuitively possessed by believers. At the same time, this 20th verse states the ground upon which believers are assured of the facts mentioned in verses 18 and 19, as to their relationship with God and their consequent condition regarding sin, Satan and the world.

In stressing again, and finally, the Divine relationship imparted to believers, the Apostle recalls the truths of the pre-existence of the Son of God and His Incarnation. The perfect tenses indicate the permanent results of what is stated.

and hath given us an understanding,—*Dianoia* ("understanding") signifies a process of mind leading to a conclusion, and hence the word denotes the faculty of forming a conclusion from certain facts. The special points in which this faculty is exercised are due to the Incarnation and Death of Christ. The Apostle John does not use the word *dianoia* elsewhere.

that we know Him that is true,—"Know" is here *ginōskō*, which stresses the appropriation of knowledge rather than the possession of it (*oida*); the present tense, too, conveys the thought of a continuous process of getting to know God. The same construction and thought are expressed in Christ's prayer in John 17: 3.

This power and process of the knowledge of God through the understanding given to us, is set in contrast to the darkness of the world (verse 19); cp. Eph. 4: 18), and in contrast to the claims of the Gnostics, who regarded the Christian faith as merely an effort to communicate with the Infinite. The believer is not groping in the dark.

For the singificance of *alēthinos*, "true", see on 2: 8,—true as opposed to what is spurious and unreal, not true as opposed to what is false (which would be expressed by *alēthēs*). Again, God is not only the source of truth, He is the one and only genuine God.

and we are in Him that is true,—That is not expressed as a purpose but as a distinct fact. The reference is again to the Father. The increasing knowledge of Him that is true is possible because we are in Him. The relationship involves the knowledge.

even in His Son Jesus Christ.—There is no need for the italicized addition "even." The point is that, being in the Father, we are in the Son, and, *vice versa*, being in the Son, we are in the Father. Both facts are intimated; the one involves the other; for what is stressed in the whole statement is the essential unity of the Father and the Son (cp. John 10: 30; 14: 9, 10). What is predicated of the Father is here likewise predicated of the Son. Thus the essential Deity of Christ is declared.

This (the undivided, indivisible Father and Son) *is the true God,*— Attempts to make the "This" refer either to the Father or to the Son fall short of what seems to be intended, namely, the inseparable unity of the Father and the Son in the one Godhead.

God is not an abstract conception, existing in the minds of people who hold certain doctrines, He is a Personal reality, revealed in and through the Son, and experienced personally by believers.

and eternal life.—Lit., "life eternal", with stress on each word. The experience just referred to, in the preceding note, is summed up in this. Christ is the embodiment, as well as the source, of the life which springs from God and is given to believers, and will for ever be ministered to them. To have the life is to have the Person in eternal possession (5: 12). The Apostle has stated that "God is light" (1: 5) and that "God is love" (4: 8, 16); he now says, in effect, that "God is life." At the same time he recalls his opening phrase "concerning the Word of life" (1: 1), which forms his great subject.

VERSE 21. **My little children,**—See at 2: 1, 12, 28; 3: 7, 18; 4: 4. The address is to all the readers.

guard yourselves—*Phulassō*, stronger than *tēreō*, "to keep." The aorist, or point tense, here signifies the decisiveness of the command; there is to be no hesitation, no wavering; the command is to be constantly carried out, and at every point wholeheartedly fulfilled.

from idols.—If we would enjoy the practical experience of being in the Father and in the Son, we must guard ourselves against the perils that arise from a world lying in the evil one. An idol is not only a heathen image; the literal significance of the word "idol" is "what is seen"; it signifies not only that which would engage the attention of the physical eyesight, to the detriment of the use of our spiritual faculties, but also any false conception which would engross the mind to the obscuring of the vision of faith. We are to guard ourselves against everything that would mar the spiritual life which Christ would live out in us, everything of self which would interrupt the power and effect of that life, every teaching which masquerades as truth, but which on spiritual examination is found to contain that which is contrary to Scripture, and therefore denies in any measure the attributes of God, the One God, Father, Son and Holy Spirit.

THE SECOND EPISTLE OF JOHN

Introduction

The question as to whom this Epistle is addressed has been the subject of much conjecture. Two views which are chiefly held, that it is addressed either to a special community or church, or to some lady known personally to the Apostle. The arguments that have been advanced in favour of one view or the other show that dogmatism is to be avoided. Since the withholding of the facts was evidently intentional, any endeavour to establish them seems inadvisable. For some reason or other the Apostle purposely refrained from disclosing both his own name and the identity of the person or the community whom he was addressing as well as that of the person or community spoken of as "thy elect sister." The disclosure might have involved some form of persecution, or the danger of the times may have led to the Apostle's decision in these respects. The recipient or recipients would have no difficulty in recognising the writer and the other detail. As to "the elder" there is little difficulty about regarding him as the Apostle John. These and other details are referred to in the Notes.

ANALYSIS

Notes

VERSE 1. **The elder unto the elect lady and her children,**—The elder we may safely assume to be the Apostle John. The word does not signify mere age, it indicates a spiritual position and care. "The elect lady" is, lit., "an elect lady", but the rendering with the definite article may be right. If the reference is to an individual, the phrase may be a general description, or the word rendered "lady" maybe a proper name, "kyria"; some regard "Electra" also as a proper name, but this seems unlikely. If the elect lady is a church, her children would be the members of the church.

whom I love—The "I" is emphatic, and possibly this indicates a condition of controversy with which the Apostle had to contend. If so it may have had something to do with the comparative privacy of the personal details of the Epistle.

in truth;—Not " in the truth", as in the A.V., as if the reference was to doctrine. The absence of the article here indicates the meaning "in the sphere of truth", that is, in all sincerity, in contrast to a profession of love that was actually hypocritical.

and not I only, but also all they that know the truth;—Lit., "they that have come to know" (cp. 1 John 2: 3). All such enjoy that communion the very element of which is mutual love. "The truth" here signifies that which is summed up, embodied and revealed in Christ, who is Himself "the truth" (John 14: 6; cp. 1: 17).

for the truth's sake—This goes with "whom I love." The love is not mere sentiment, as if it was due to the attractiveness of its objects; its very foundation is the truth, that is, the truth which finds its full expression in Christ.

which abideth in us,—See John 15: 4-10, and especially the Lord's command, "If ye abide in Me, and My words abide in you" (vv. 4 and 7). The Holy Spirit, "the Spirit of truth", puts great stress upon the truth in this and the Third Epistles of John. The popular religion of the present day is that, provided you exercise love, differences of opinion do not matter, and we must agree to differ. That is not the mind of the Lord. His command is that we should be "thoroughly joined together in the same mind, and in the same judgment." The truth of God's Word must never be surrendered to the sentiment of love, all important as it is that we should love one another (see ver. 6). The truth makes love possible.

and it shall be with us for ever.—The Apostle passes from desire to assurance. There is emphasis on "with us." In this verse the same two prepositions are used of the truth as in John 14: 16, 17 concerning the Holy Spirit, and the promise "for ever" is made in each. The prepositions are *meta*, the "with" of intimate accompaniment (John 14: 16 and here), and *en*, the "in" of indwelling (John 14:17 and here). In John 14 a third is used, namely, *para*, the "with" of support (John 14: 17). As with the Spirit so with the truth, each exercises a living power and through Christ a Personal power.

VERSE 3. **Grace, mercy, peace shall be with us,**—The language of assurance in verse 2 is continued in this verse. The former has perhaps influenced the latter. The same threefold Divine blessing, grace, mercy, peace, is used in the salutations in 1 and 2 Timothy and Titus, and used for individuals, whereas in Paul's Epistles to churches the words grace and peace are usual. Peter in both his Epistles says "Grace and peace be multiplied." Jude says "Mercy unto you and peace and love be multiplied."

The three words comprehend God's gracious dealings with man. Grace is God's favour shown to man, free and unmerited. Mercy is the active manifestation of pity toward those who are in need. Grace is God's attitude toward the sinful, mercy is His attitude toward those in distress. His grace precedes His mercy. Peace is the result to all who receive God's favour in Christ. Peace describes both the harmonized relationship between God and those who through faith become His children (John 1:12; Acts 10: 36), and the sense of rest and contentment consequent thereon (John 14: 27; Rom. 1: 7; 3: 17; 8: 6).

from God the Father, and from Jesus Christ,—That the three blessings just mentioned come alike from God the Father and from Jesus Christ is a testimony to the Deity of Christ. At the same time the repetition of the preposition "from" marks the distinct Personality of the Father and of the Son. This anticipates the errors which the Apostle is about to expose (vv. 7 and 10).

the Son of the Father,—This is the only place in the N.T. where this especial title is used. It is designed here to lay stress upon the great foundation truth that the Incarnate Son of God is the Person through whom the Father has revealed Himself to men.

in truth and love.—These two words are the dominant notes of this Epistle. Truth is in the sphere of thought, love is in the sphere of action. The genuineness of the one expresses itself in the practice of the other. We are to abide steadfastly in the truth and manifest the love which springs from it. Grace, mercy and peace come from the Father through the Son in both respects.

VERSE 4. **I rejoice greatly**—The tense of the verb is the aorist, or past definite. Since Greek writers were accustomed to use that tense in letter writing where we should use the present (see Note on the First Epistle, 5: 13), the R.V. rendering is rightly that of the epistolary aorist. It is possible that this past tense refers to a previous occasion on which he found what he here states, but, inasmuch as his joy was not merely then but continued up to the time of writing, it is better to render by the present tense, "I rejoice." Cp. 3 John 3, R.V. margin.

that I have found certain of thy children walking in truth,—Not that he had been seeking it, but that on visiting a certain locality he found the believers he mentions walking in such a spiritual way. It is not necessary to gather that only some of the children were walking in truth while others were not doing so. The Apostle may have come across only some of them. The fact that he speaks afterwards about false teachers does not necessarily imply that they had led astray some of the children.

For *peripateō*, used of the conduct of the life, see 1 John 1:" For "in truth", *i.e.*, in the sphere of truth, see verse 1.

even as we received commandment from the Father.—The expression "even as" indicates the entirety of their obedience (cp. 1 John

2: 6, 27; 3: 3, 7, 23; 4: 17). The use of the aorist tense here points to the direct decisive way in which the commandment came and was received. For the prominence which the Apostle gives in the 1st and 2nd Epistles to the word "commandment" see 1 John 2: 7, 8. It is used four times in this passage. The commandment was given for obedience and came from the Father. All that the Son heard from the Father He made known to His disciples (John 15: 15).

Love, truth and obedience are connected. Love without obedience is mere sentiment, and lacks reality. Obedience without love is mere servility. Love and obedience must be founded on, and directed by, truth. Truth finds its expression and activity in love; they form together (and they are found together here only in the N.T.) a doctrinal and a moral harmony.

VERSE 5.   **And now I beseech thee, lady,**—While this introduces an exhortation, it is connected with what precedes. The mode of request is as from an equal to an equal, owing to their oneness in Christ and their common relationship to him.

not as though I wrote to thee a new commandment, but that which we had from the beginning,—That is, not as if it were a fresh commandment, new in kind (*kainos*, as distinct from *neos*, new in time). "From the beginning" probably means from the beginning of our experience of the Lord's teaching.

that we love one another,—This is probably to be taken both with "I beseech thee" and with the commandment.

VERSE 6.   **And this is love, that we should walk after His commandments.**—That is to say, love consists in this. The "this is" links the definition to the request (v. 5). The plural expresses the attitude of love in general; it consists in the fulfilment of all God's will. In verse 5, the new commandment is that we love one another; in verse 6 love is the fulfilment of the commandment. Thus in verse 5 obedience finds its expression in love; in verse 6 love finds its expression in obedience. The former is contrary to mere pious sentiment; the latter, is contrary to mere servility. "After" means "according to." Cp. Rom. 8: 4; 2 Cor: 10: 2.

The order of the words, commandment . . . love, love . . . commandments (vv. 5, 6) is chiastic [(a), (b), (b), (a)], a frequent mode of Scripture statements and instruction.

This is the commandment, even as ye heard from the beginning, that ye should walk in it,—The commandment here is again that "we love one another" and the "it" at the end of the sentence refers probably to this love, for that it is in which the commandment consists. The Apostle does not speak elsewhere of walking "in" a commandment or "in" commandments; he has just spoken of walking "after" commandments. Paul speaks of walking in love (Eph. 5: 2). "From the beginning" here refers to the times when they were first taught the Christian faith and became believers; for he is now not including himself but addressing them.

VERSE 7. **For many deceivers are gone forth into the world,**— This gives one great reason, not for the injunction in verse 8 but for the preceding instruction as to true Christian love, walking "in truth" and after the Lord's commandments. All this provides a safeguard against error, and its deceptive propagators. The word rendered "deceivers" signifies imposters of the vagabond type, and hence any kind of corrupter (cp. Matt. 27: 63; 2 Cor. 6: 8); it is used of "seducing" spirits in 1 Tim. 4: 1. It is not used elsewhere in the N.T.

The R.V. "are gone forth" translates the most authentic MSS., instead of the A.V., "are entered." It seems likely that these seducers had been assembling with the churches and had gone forth from them spreading their evil doctrines in the world. They went forth for the purpose of promulgating their heresy. Compare what the Apostle says about the antichrists in the First Epistle, 2: 18, 19: "they went out from us, but they were not of us"; and now he speaks similarly of one who teaches the special error mentioned.

even they that confess not that Jesus Christ cometh in the flesh.— Not to confess is the same thing as denying. The truth which these deceivers denied is not accurately stated either in the A.V., that Jesus Christ "is come", or in the R.V., that He "cometh." It is necessary here to translate the original by the English equivalent of the Greek present participle: "even they that confess not Jesus Christ coming in flesh." That is to say, the denial was a denial both of the fact of the Incarnation and of its possibility at any time, including the future Coming when we shall see Him "even as He is" (1 John 3: 2).

This rejection of the possibility that God could become manifest in the flesh shows traces of Gnosticism, which had influenced Judaism and had crept into the churches. Hence arose these deceivers, who taught that matter is essentially evil, and that therefore God could not associate Himself with evil flesh by incarnation, and that Christ was indeed Divine, but His body was a phantom. They promulgated the view that real Christianity was to be understood intellectually, and that their teaching was thus superior to any such view as that Christ had come or ever could come in flesh.

Their teaching thus struck at the great essential of God's way of salvation and true Christianity, both in doctrine and practice. False teaching ever begets evil doing.

The truth of the Incarnation was a special battle ground in the early churches, and though, through such faithful and assiduous defence of the faith and through attacks upon such apostates as are in evidence in these Epistles of the Apostle John, the truth triumphed in those days, yet the sword has still to be wielded in defence of this great essential of Christian doctrine.

This is the deceiver and the antichrist.—The definite articles (which have been suppressed in the A.V.) are important. What has been stated by way of a general description is now individualized. "This is" sets a definite stamp upon the errorist. Whatever additional characteristics there are of teachers of this false doctrine, this is decisive. In the capacity of "the deceiver" the evil teacher acts against man: in his capacity as "the antichrist" he acts against God. An antichrist, as a precursor of the coming Antichrist, is not only opposed to Christ, he aims at usurping His authority (cp. the two ideas in 2 Thess. 2: 3).

VERSE 8.   **Look to yourselves,**—The craft of the opponents of the truth demands self-examination, a watchfulness against being contaminated in the slightest degree.

that ye lose not the things which we have wrought, but that ye receive a full reward.—The "we" refers to the Apostle and others who brought them the gospel and taught them the ways of the Lord. The warning against losing, and the exhortation as to receiving a full reward, point to the Judgment-seat of Christ, where each one "will receive the things done in the body, according to what he hath done, whether it be good or bad" (2 Cor. 5: 10). Each person's work will be "made manifest . . . if any man's work shall abide . . . he shall receive a reward. If any man's work shall be burned, he shall suffer loss" (1 Cor. 3: 15-15). See also Col. 3: 24, 25. To turn away from the faith, or to depart from the path of loyalty to Christ and of moral rectitude, will result in eternal and utterly regrettable loss. To abide in Christ and remain faithful to the end will bring an eternal and joyous reward. "If we endure, we shall also reign with Him: if we shall deny Him, He also will deny us" (2 Tim. 2: 11, 12). See also Rev. 22: 12. Such loss will bring sorrow to those who have brought us to Christ and led us spiritually according to the Scriptures. That is what the Apostle has in view in this passage. A "full" reward is that in which nothing is wanting.

VERSE 9. **Whosoever goeth onward and abideth not in the teaching of Christ, hath not God:**—The R.V., "goeth onward" follows the most authentic MSS. It was a sarcastic reference to the professed higher knowledge of the false teachers. This meaning became misunderstood, and hence a copyist thought fit to change the word to one meaning "transgresseth." The significance of the word, rightly rendered "goeth onward", is not that of progress itself, but an advance in teaching that goes beyond the teaching of Christ; that is to say, not only the teaching concerning the Person of Christ, but that which He gave and commanded His followers to teach. Anyone who goes beyond this, the Apostle declares, "hath not God" (*i.e.*, as his God), however much He may claim to know Him. For "teaching" cp. 1 John 2: 22 to 24 and see John 18: 19; Acts 2: 42; Rev. 2: 14, 15. There may be great professions of religion and religious zeal, but to add to, or depart from, the teaching of Christ (as Jude calls it, "the faith once for all delivered to the saints", R.V.) must eventually involve that condemnation which He foretold when He said, "Then will I profess unto them, I never knew you: depart from Me, ye that work iniquity" (or rather, "lawlessness"; that is, whatever is contrary to the will of God).

he that abideth in the teaching, the same hath both the Father and the Son.—The phrase "he that abideth" translates the definite article with the present participle of the verb, which more precisely defines a person as being characterized by what is stated. The change from "hath not God" to "hath the Father and the Son", shows that truly to possess God is to possess both the Father and the Son, the two being one in Godhood.

VERSE 10. **If any one cometh unto you,**—The conjunction "if", in the original, does not express a supposition or possibility, as the A.V. rendering implies, it assumes a fact (as in John 7: 4, 23; 8: 39,

46; 18: 8; 1 John 5: 9). The "cometh" does not imply a visit, it here signifies a coming as a teacher (cp. 3 John 10), advancing his own ideas.

and bringeth not this teaching,—The negative (*ou* not *mē*) has a special emphasis, serving to distinguish in a very definite way the false teacher from faithful believers. The statement marks the test of fellowship.

receive him not into your house, and give him no greeting:—This excludes all manner of welcome. The injunctions are a faithful prohibition against compromising the truth. For a professed teacher, who is actually a propagator of an error which strikes at a foundation truth of the faith, and therefore is not a Christian, to be received into a believer's house as if the errorist was himself a believer, firstly, is disloyalty to Christ, secondly, makes it possible for him to do incalculable harm to the saints, thirdly, tends to establish him in his false teaching, and, fourthly, means personal fellowship in the evil by condoning false doctrine (v. 11). The suggestion that we are living in times when the Apostle's uncompromising attitude is scarcely applicable, is to be regarded as utterly fallacious, and to be repudiated as dangerous. Errors relating to the Person and work of Christ have multiplied, and have increased in their subtle speciousness. Accordingly, fidelity to Christ demands obedience to the commands here given, and forbids the slightest toleration of both the teachings and the teachers. Love of the truth involves hatred of error.

VERSE 11. **For he that giveth him greeting partaketh in his evil works.**—Participation does not adequately express the meaning of *koinōneō*, which signifies to have fellowship with. The A.V. "deeds" is inadequate; *ergon* is a work, and has a wider meaning than a deed. Teaching is a work and is more than an act, and the work of false teaching is what the Apostle is here speaking of.

VERSE 12. **Having many things to write unto you,**—The verb *graphō*, to write, which ordinarily denotes to write by letter etc., may be used in the wider sense of communicating in other ways, and that may possibly be the meaning here.

I would not write them with paper and ink:—The word *chartēs* (whence Eng. chart, charter) is used here only in the N.T. It signifies a sheet of paper made of strips of papyrus, which was abundant in the Nile and was formed into a material for writing.*

Ink (*melan*, black) is mentioned elsewhere in 2 Cor. 3: 3 and 3 John 13.

but I hope to come unto you,—Lit., to become (*i.e.*, be) with you; *pros*, with, denotes more than company (as in the case of *meta* and *sun*), it indicates the enjoyment of presence and attitude (cp. John 1: 1, 2). The "you" is plural, and includes the children mentioned in verse 1.

and to speak face to face,—Lit., mouth to mouth, which is used especially of speaking together; in 1 Cor. 13: 12 the phrase is "face to face" (*prosōpon*, a word which originally signified eye).

that your joy may be fulfilled.—See on 1 John 1: 4.

VERSE 13. **The children of thine elect sister salute thee.**—That the salutation is sent from the children affords no absolute proof that the elect lady is a church. The nephews may not have been in the same place as their mother at the time.

* See the author's *Expository Dictionary of New Testament Words*, section Vol. III, p. 157.

THE THIRD EPISTLE OF JOHN

Introduction

This is a private Epistle to an individual and affords no room from such differences of opinion in this respect as in the addressee of the First Epistle. The Apostle speaks in the same authoritative tone as in the previous Epistle, but this is a letter of encouragement rather than of warning. The Second Epistle contends against false teaching; the Third condemns schism.

The name Gaius was so common in the Roman Empire that it serves no useful purpose to try and identify the one to whom this Epistle is addressed with any of the other three (or perhaps two) mentioned elsewhere in the N.T. Again it is quite precarious to seek to identify the Demetrius of verse 12 with the silversmith in Ephesus, on the supposition that he was converted subsequently to his opposition to Paul.

Analysis

Notes

VERSE 1. **The elder unto Gaius the beloved,**—For the opening words see on 2 John 1. For "Gaius" see the Introductory Note above. The Apostle calls him "beloved" four times (vv. 1, 2, 5, 11). See also 1 John 2: 7; 3: 2, 21; 4: 1, 7, 11. There is no formal greeting here, it is practically contained in verse 2.

whom I love in truth.—See on 2 John 1. The "I" is emphatic. Perhaps this implies insincerity on the part of others, or even antagonism.

VERSE 2. **Beloved, I pray that in all things**—The preposition *peri*, here rendered "in", denotes "concerning"; it does not denote "above", as in the A.V. Moreover the Apostle would not wish Gaius prosperity and health "above" all things. The meaning is "respecting all things", *i.e.*, 'in all respects', and this goes with "thou mayest prosper and be in health."

thou mayest prosper and be in health,—The verb *euodoumai*, lit., means to have a good journey, but it came to denote to prosper in any way. It is used elsewhere in the N.T. in Rom. 1: 10 and 1 Cor. 16: 2. The verb *hugiainō*, to be in health (Eng. hygiene), is used of physical fitness. This does not imply that Gaius was in poor health or was suffering poverty; it certainly provides an example of, and encouragement to, prayer for material blessings for fellow-believers.

even as thy soul prospereth.—This indicates the good desire that the circumstances of a believer such as Gaius may correspond to his spiritual prosperity. How he prospered in soul is seen in what the Apostle now records of him. The spiritual life is to be uppermost, but the material affairs are not ignored. If the material dominates the spiritual, the consequences are disastrous and the way is prepared for backsliding. The soul, the immaterial part of man's being is that which lives the higher life, and in the case of the spiritually minded believer is, together with the body, energized by the Spirit of God. See Heb. 6: 19; 10: 39; 13: 17; 1 Pet. 2: 11; 4: 19.

VERSE 3. **For I rejoiced greatly,**—Cp. 2 John 4, but this in verse 3 is not the epistolary aorist.

when brethren came and bare witness—Not "the brethren"; there is no definite article. No specially appointed brethren came to give the report. Moreover, the verbs are in the present participle, possibly indicating that there were occasional visits or visits by more than one company. Literally, the statement could be rendered 'I rejoiced greatly at brethren coming and witnessing."

unto thy truth,—That is, to his faithfulness in maintaining the Christian faith in his life and conduct.

even as thou walkest in truth.—Cp. 2 John 4. The "thou" is emphatic; it is suggested that this is set in contrast to the conduct of Diotrephes. To walk in truth is to love according to the teaching and standard of the doctrines of the faith as revealed by God. This last statement is an intimation of the Apostle's knowledge of, and joy in, him.

VERSE 4.   **Greater joy have I none than this,**—For *charis*, joy, see 2 John 3. In the most authentic texts the "this" is plural, "these things", referring to that which he has mentioned, namely, the reports given by visiting brethren, as summed up in what follows.

to hear of my children walking in the truth.—Or rather, "my own children", the pronoun "my" being in a position of emphasis; it indicates that they were brought to a saving knowledge of Christ through the Apostle himself. "The truth" here signifies all the doctrines of the faith, and that as embodied and manifested in Christ, Himself "The Truth." To walk in the truth is to live the life of the true follower of Christ, in all the activities of Christian conduct, a life of progress towards a goal. The Apostle Paul expresses it thus: "To me living is Christ" (Phil. 1: 21).

VERSE 5.   **Beloved, thou doest a faithful work in whatsoever thou doest**—The original is, literally, "thou doest a faithful thing whatsoever thou workest." There is no noun "work" in the first part of the statement. The first verb is *poieō* ("thou doest"); the second is *ergazomai*, to work (the same verb as that rendered "wrought" in 2 John 8). The same two verbs are used together in Col. 3: 23. The meaning seems to be somewhat as follows: "In the work you are doing on behalf of brethren you are acting faithfully", (or it may be, "what you are doing is an expression of the faith that characterizes you." Westcott translates it "Thou makest sure whatsoever thou workest." That is, such work will be sure of a reward. The "whatsoever" suggests a variety of service.

toward them that are brethren and strangers withal;—The construction in the original is the same as that in Matt. 26: 10, "she hath wrought a good work upon Me." The preposition *eis* is better rendered "toward." The "brethren" and "strangers" are the same persons. Spiritually related to him by the ties of the new birth, those whom he entertained had been unknown to him personally. This enhances the value of his recognition of them as fellow-believers.

VERSE 6. **who bare witness to thy love before the church:**—The preceding statement spoke of his faith; this declares his love. Love is the outworking of faith. This was evidence of the prosperity of his soul. The church was the assembly of believers where the Apostle was when he wrote.

whom thou wilt do well to set forward on their journey worthily of God:—Having commended Gaius for his hospitality shown to these servants of God, John encourages him to assist them on their way. The form of verb rendered "to set forward on their journey" is the aorist participle (more lit., "having set forward") and indicates especially the decisiveness and completeness of the act, viewing it not as a process nor even as a past act. The phrase "worthily of God" signifies "in a manner consistent with their devotedness to the service of God." Cp. 1 Thess. 2: 12; Col. 1: 10. See John 13: 20.

VERSE 7. **because that for the sake of the Name they went forth,**— The most authentic texts have simply "the Name" (not His Name). Cp. Acts 5: 41, R.V., The Name is that of the Lord Jesus. His Name expresses all that He is, His character and attributes as seen in His doings, and therefore is summed up in all the doctrines concerning Him, His Deity, His eternal Sonship, His sinless Life, His Death, Resurrection and exalted position at the right hand of the Throne. All these and more are wrapped up in the Name "Jesus." See Phil. 2: 9.

That they "went forth" indicates the missionary spirit, and the way in which the Lord thrust forth, and is thrusting forth, labourers in the "harvest field of the world."

taking nothing of the Gentiles.—They refused to seek help for their needs from unbelievers. Their dependence was upon God for all the requirements of their service. The verb rendered "taking" is in the present participle, indicating that what is said was their regular custom. Accordingly, there was need for the assistance of men like Gaius. It was not that the Gentiles offered help and were refused, but that the servants of God refrained from asking for their help. The facts are recorded for the guidance both of missionaries at all times, and of those who, not being called to go forth, have the responsibility and privilege of co-operation with them by rendering practical assistance "worthily of God." The loyal fulfilment of this co-operation makes us, what is mentioned in verse 8, "fellow-workers with the truth." Neglect to render this assistance must meet with the disapproval of "the Lord of the harvest."

VERSE 8. **We therefore ought to welcome such,**—The "we" is emphatic, marking a contrast to the Gentiles. The verb rendered "to welcome" is *hupolambanō*, and there is perhaps a play upon the preceding verb *lambanō*, to take. As the missionaries refused to *take* from Gentiles, others ought to *undertake* for such servants of God. The word does not mean merely to receive (as in the A.V.) but to welcome, and that as only part of the co-operation.

that we may be fellow-workers with the truth.—Lit., "to the truth", or "for the truth", that is to say, "fellow-workers with them for the truth", thus supporting the truth in its effectiveness through their instrumentality. Cp. 1 Cor. 9: 23, R.V., and Col. 4: 11.

VERSE 9. **I wrote somewhat unto the church:**—This refers, not to the Second Epistle, but to a brief letter which does not exist and which may have been suppressed by Diotrephes.

but Diotrephes, who loveth to have the pre-eminence among them, receiveth us not.—The verb *philoprōteuō*, to "love being pre-eminent", is used here only in the N.T. Diotrephes was in the assembly and a man of prominence, but he was guilty in four respects: (1) an ambition to hold the chief place, (2) a refusal to receive John and his fellow-workers, (3) slanderous attacks upon them, (4) excommunicating those who would receive them.

VERSE 10. **Therefore, if I come,**—This is not a supposition, it signifies that his presence will be decisive.

I will bring to remembrance his works that he doeth,—That is to say, he would draw the attention of the whole assembly to the matter. Contrast verse 6. The two ideas of doing and works are in direct contrast here to the commendatory approval of Gaius in verse 5. The verb *hupomimnēskō*, to bring to mind, is used with various objects, in Luke 22: 61; John 14: 26; 2 Tim. 2: 14; Tit. 3: 1; Jude 5.

prating against us with wicked words:—The verb *phluareō*, here only in the N.T., has the meaning of making false accusations in a garrulous way. The word *ponēros*, evil, is the same as in 2 John 11, and as in the phrase "the evil one" (1 John 2: 13, where see Note).

and not content therewith, neither doth he himself receive the brethren,—The verb *epidechomai*, to receive, is used only in verse 9 and here in the N.T.; it here signifies to give hospitality.

and them that would be forbiddeth, and casteth them out of the church.—This was the utmost height of autocratic exclusiveness. Diotrephes refused fellowship with, and thus excommunicated, those who desired to receive them. The present continuous tense in the verbs does not seem merely to indicate an endeavour to forbid and cast out, it expresses a regular course of action. Self-seeking may attain to success, but it issues in futility and incurs Divine judgment.

VERSE 11. **Beloved, imitate not that which is evil, but that which is good.**—The term "beloved" marks, as before, the introduction of a change in the message, and yet there is this connection, that the evils of Diotrephes afford the basis of a gracious exhortation and moral application.

The verb *mimeomai* is used three times elsewhere in positive exhortations, 2 Thess. 3: 7, 9; Heb. 13: 7. The word rendered "evil" here is the general term *kakos*; there is no purposive contrast to *ponēros* in v. 10.

He that doeth good is of God:—The doing is habitual, not a specific act, and the believer whose life consists in doing good shows that he is born of (*ek*) God and has God as the Source of his manner of life. See 1 John 2: 29; 3: 9; 4: 6, 7, and Notes on these passages.

he that doeth evil hath not seen God.—See Notes on 1 John 3: 6. These statements have a wide and general reference and do not merely refer to the matters of which the Apostle has been writing. The evildoer has not entered the very beginning of Divine relationship. The vision of faith is the first step of communion with God.

VERSE 12. **Demetrius hath the witness of all men,**—Possibly he was the bearer of this letter. The suggestion that this is the Demetrius of Acts 19: 24 is mere conjecture and improbable. Lit., the rendering is "Witness hath been borne (the perfect tense signifying a complete and abiding effect) to Demetrius by all", that is, by all who knew him and especially those of the assembly to which he belonged and the brethren who were mentioned in verse 5. He no doubt also had a good report of "them that are without." This statement by the Apostle is set as the standard of life and conduct for all believers.

and of the truth itself:—His life corresponded to the truth of Scripture and therefore was directed by "the Spirit of Truth" (1 John 5: 6), the truth thus vindicating his conduct. The effect of this would also be that his conscience was happily confirmatory of the truth.

yea, we also bear witness;—See on 1 John 1: 2, and cp. John 15: 27; Acts 5: 32. There was a threefold testimony to Demetrius.

and thou knowest that our witness is true.—Gaius himself was so well known to, and so joyously acquainted with, Demetrius that he was well aware (*oida*, to know completely and intuitively) of the fact mentioned by the Apostle. Cp. John 21: 24.

VERSE 13.   **I had many things to write unto thee,**—The imperfect tense here signifies that at the time of writing he had many things to say. We should say "I have many things to say."

but I am unwilling to write them to thee with ink and pen:—Compare and contrast 2 John 12. The *kalamos*, a reed (which has several meanings) is used of a writing reed or pen here only. It was used for writing on papyrus and leather. Metal pens of very ancient times have been discovered. The quill pen (not referred to here) is first mentioned in the 5th century, A.D.

VERSE 14.   **But I hope shortly to see thee, and we shall speak face to face.**—The adverb *eutheōs* means "straightway", not "shortly", which does not signify sufficiently soon. Cp. 2 John 12.

Peace be unto thee.—This common mode of greeting or farewell among the Jews became enriched in its use among believers owing to the effect of the words of the Lord recorded in John 14: 27; 20: 19, 26.

The friends salute thee.—That is, the believers where the Apostle was, and as known to Gaius. *Philos*, a friend, conveys the thoughts of intimacy and affection.

Salute the friends by name.—That is, each one. The phrase "by name" is used elsewhere in the N.T. only in John 10: 3. The Apostle may have had the Lord's words in mind, himself entering into the spirit of an under-shepherd.

DATE DUE